be a brilliant entrepreneur

Alex McMillan

For UK order enquiries: please contact Bookpoint Ltd,
130 Milton Park, Abingdon, Oxon OX14 4SB.
Telephone: +44 (0) 1235 827720. *Fax*: +44 (0) 1235 400454.
Lines are open 09.00–17.00, Monday to Saturday, with a
24-hour message answering service. Details about our titles
and how to order are available at www.hoddereducation.com

British Library Cataloguing in Publication Data: a catalogue
record for this title is available from the British Library.

This edition published 2011 by Hodder Education, part of
Hachette UK, 338 Euston Road, London NW1 3BH.

Typeset by MPS Limited, a Macmillan Company.

Printed in Great Britain for Hodder Education, an Hachette UK Company,
338 Euston Road, London NW1 3BH, by CPI Cox & Wyman, Reading,
Berkshire RG1 8EX.

The publisher has used its best endeavours to ensure that the URLs for
external websites referred to in this book are correct and active at the time of
going to press. However, the publisher and the author have no responsibility
for the websites and can make no guarantee that a site will remain live or
that the content will remain relevant, decent or appropriate.

Hachette UK's policy is to use papers that are natural, renewable and
recyclable products and made from wood grown in sustainable forests.
The logging and manufacturing processes are expected to conform to the
environmental regulations of the country of origin.

Impression number   10 9 8 7 6 5 4 3 2 1
Year   2015 2014 2013 2012 2011

Contents

1

what if your entrepreneur dream happened?

Only one in a hundred people with an entrepreneur dream actually make it happen. I wonder what the other 99 could have achieved, invented, developed, innovated, created, inspired, changed for the better and how much money they would have made. Be a 1%er.

The stopper is not lack of ideas or finance, but determination to make it happen.

Every company in Britain from one man bands to the FTSE100 was started by someone just like you. They had an idea, a passion and the belief to see it through. They had the true grit to make the jump, to be all they could be. If you are any good at anything, chances are someone is paying you now and selling your talent for a margin. My advice, work for yourself, make your dream happen, and make it now.

A few years from now

You made it. You finally escaped the rat race – built yourself a business to become financially free. You now have the choice to continue and grow or sell out and take a capital gain, enough to retire on.

Imagine now going to estate agents to choose your ideal house with all of the facilities and features you always dreamed about. You tell the agent the location you had in mind: perhaps in this country, perhaps abroad, you know the one. You have waited a while for it to be ready and you are going to pick up the keys now and pay for it in cash. As you walk up the front drive, you feel absolutely fabulous on what you see as the first day of how you always wanted to live with everything you have always wanted. The house is just the material reward; the personal satisfaction of having built a successful business gives you a buzz. You remember all those people who warned you of the risks, told you that you had a good, well-paid, secure job.

The house looks marvelous, you cannot wait to go in. You step in; yes, it looks good, feels good, it even smells good, of newness and quality. It is a beautiful day and the sun is shining. You cannot wait to take a swim in the luxury pool. As each moment passes you can feel your excitement growing.

From your favourite music selection you choose something upbeat and positive that suggests success. The feeling of excitement grows as you switch on the music. Your mind fills with images of your new villa with its breathtaking view over the sea from the hot tub. Designed to your specific requirements it is literally perfect. As you continue to enjoy your day more and more, you notice the office workers hurrying back from lunch. Not for you ever again; you are a successful entrepreneur, you are free. Your mind wanders as you take in the expected luxuries and total freedom of the weeks and months ahead.

Feeling like a million pounds, you hope secretly to pass by certain people you know, those who said you would never do it, who never gave you support when asked. You call a few close family members and friends, and invite them around for the house warming. You order chilled champagne and lie back in the pool with a big SMILE on your face. You toy over all the things you are going to indulge in over the next couple of weeks, months, years. An occasional thought wanders back to those you have left on the 7:32 to Waterloo that morning.

The most pleasant feeling though, is that of success, coupled with the rise in self-esteem and pride. It has not been easy, but you have made it. You think back to your moments of doubt and hesitation, thankful that you did not give up or chicken out. You think back over the obstacles you overcame and feel very proud of your success. You also think of those you love the most and what you are now able to do for them.

Americans call the above 'dreambuilding'. Write down what you would want when you have achieved success, then go out and taste it now. By doing this your mind sets up the future you are working towards. Involve all your senses to achieve a real sensation. Go out and visit your dream house, test drive your dream car, look at brochures for your holiday of a lifetime. The taster gives firm images of what motivates you, making them real: a sort of future memory. Research has found that this simple idea is not only pleasant, it does increase motivation and focus and keeps you on track to achieve the future you desire.

You will never have to work again, although you probably will want to, as you love your work. What you have worked for has turned from a dream to reality. For the next week at least you are going to soak up the reality on the beach, in the finest restaurants, with someone special to you. You are going to spend and spend: fashionable designer clothes, made to measure, parties, sports. You ponder a while on what you want to buy, knowing that money is no object now. Those months of focusing your money on investments ensure that your 'pot of gold' is constantly refilled and you can now afford to indulge yourself and still grow your wealth.

What is an entrepreneur?

People have different understandings of the term 'entrepreneur'. The motives of an entrepreneur are numerous: some are purely focused on making money; some are totally focused on developing their innovations, and money is just the mechanism that allows it to happen, or even a side effect of success. Most entrepreneurs are after both. So when is an entrepreneur successful? Does making more money make an entrepreneur more successful? What do you think? Part of being an entrepreneur is doing your own thinking, making your own decisions!

There are two distinct aspects of an entrepreneur.

1 Someone, who through creativity, innovation, foresight and discovery, can identify commercial opportunities around him or her.

2 Someone practical who sees and exploits opportunities for making money successfully.

This includes the self-employed, small business owners, those embarking on setting up their own business, investors, artists, software writers, inventors, authors and songwriters.

In many successful enterprises these two elements are often found in two people. This is not surprising as practicality and creativity can, but certainly not necessarily, be opposites. In both cases, practicality and creativity are skills you can acquire from these pages. I will show you how to set yourself up to recognize opportunities that you are currently missing. Then comes the practical steps you must go through to turn these ideas into profit.

You have an entrepreneurial dream and wish to progress to the next level. You may not have even started in sales terms, but the idea is there or perhaps just the determination or desire. This means you have the spirit of an entrepreneur and that flame of enterprise needs to be nurtured and grown to a glowing furnace of fun and success.

How to see the world differently

An entrepreneur sees things that others miss. They can see resources or potential resources that can be used or utilized in a more beneficial, more profitable, way than they are being used now. It is the cornerstone on which capitalistic society is based.

I asked corporate executives seeking a new corporate executive position.

How do you see a corporate executive position?
   1 Security
   2 Comfort
   3 High status
   4 Professional experience
   5 Maintain high mortgage on home
   6 Good pension
   7 Training
   8 Interesting work

How do you see self-employment/entrepreneurship?
   1 Insecure, home at risk
   2 Danger and vulnerability
   3 No regular salary
   4 Most fail
   5 Independence
   6 Freedom
   7 Unlimited potential income and capital gain
   8 Early retirement if you want it

I put the same questions to a number of self-employed people/entrepreneurs:

How do you see a corporate executive position?
   1 Controlled, told what to do
   2 Regular salary and benefits
   3 A boss to report to

4 Office politics necessary to succeed and survive
5 Limited potential to grow. Not paid what worth
6 Insecure future
7 Not able to express own ideas
8 High risk, all eggs in one basket

How do you see self-employment/entrepreneurship?
1 Security
2 Financial freedom
3 Outlet for creativity
4 Independence
5 Own boss
6 Potentially unlimited income
7 Potentially unlimited capital gain
8 Paid what I am worth

In the following chapters you will find all the resources you need to become a successful entrepreneur. Expertise in the realm of, say, accounting, tax, IT and marketing can be bought in; you cannot do everything yourself.

Entrepreneurship is about deferred gratification. We have a society that has punished itself with enormous debt by seeking instant gratification. You invest now for a return in the years to come. It is about making money while you sleep. It is about developing assets that make you money without the need for your presence. It is about making a capital gain from the value you have added to a business. Employeeship is about adding value to the assets of entrepreneurs in return for the illusion of security. A regular job is instant gratification. People see it as the secure option but it can take no more than 30 seconds for the employment of a senior manager of ten years loyalty to be terminated. That is not a long-term investment. I think having ten clients is more secure than having one. I have never understood why banks still prefer to lend money to a person with only one source of income over which they have no control. I also don't understand why the system supports lending to property backed assets rather than growing businesses.

How easily can you be a successful entrepreneur?

Everyone can be a successful entrepreneur. Every entrepreneur can be a better one.

Everything you can see around you, the company you work for, every company you have ever bought something from, was created by an entrepreneur with a dream, a vision.

What stops you being an entrepreneur?

* What stops you escaping the rat race?
* What stops you starting?
* What stops you thinking of an idea?
* What stops you knowing which business to run?
* What stops you growing from a small to a large company?
* What stops you being an even better entrepreneur?

Your particular 'what is stopping you ...' question depends on where your entrepreneurial dream is right now. You need to know what stage you are at. If you are still at the dreamer stage or on the road to getting going, the question might be one of the first two in the list above.

The focus of the question is interesting in as much as it assumes that you have control, or at least can take control. This is one of the fundamental rules for successful entrepreneurship. You have to control the world around you and not let it control you. This requires strength of character. Entrepreneurship is far more about guts than brains. The beauty of this is that most really brainy people will never have the guts to launch or grow a business, so your competition is seriously reduced. That is why there are considerable opportunities for entrepreneurs. You just have to keep focusing on the goal, rather than asking 'What if it goes wrong?'

Fear – the dream thief

I believe there are a thousand ideas with the potential
of eBay, Google or Virgin that are not businesses today
because the entrepreneurs were too scared to get them off
the ground. One of my goals with this book is to release some
of the incredible potential that is in danger of remaining
bottled up.

I am not saying fear is a bad thing. On the contrary, it should
warn you of impending danger. Think ahead, prepare for every
eventuality, rather than giving up.

How to make a million

I run something called the £100K Club. At one of the
meetings I asked members of the audience the following question:
'What is the easiest way to make a million pounds?' I then asked
them to list three ways in priority order. The top answer was
winning the lottery, the second by inheritance and the third by
being an entrepreneur.

Neither of the first two answers provides me with
lasting satisfaction. I don't do the lottery: none of the prizes
appeal and there is no stimulation or competitive fun for me
in picking random numbers. Those who win the lottery often
become unhappy as it robs them of what they might have
become or achieved as a person. I don't like the idea of receiving
money from the demise of someone I love. That leaves number
three for me.

Money is often the measure but I see entrepreneurial success
in terms of adding value, giving more than you take, creativity,
innovation and fun. These are the things that give me satisfaction
and make me feel good at all levels. I have owned luxury cars, taken
exotic holidays, etc., but these are just things. So I want readers of
this book to move answer number three to number one. You have
much more control over number three.

It really is a lot easier to be a successful entrepreneur than you think. Thinking success is hard, or thinking that you won't make it can be a larger stopper of success than anything out there in the economy. In all events you can focus on the positive or the negative side. Decide which now, ahead of time, and everything that happens to you will turn to advantage. That is one of the principal secrets of entrepreneurs, what they do differently. All it requires from you is a decision.

2

what type of entrepreneur are you?

Why do you really want to be an entrepreneur? Is it to be independent, creative, make your fortune, command your own empire, perhaps all of these? You can be introvert or extrovert, risk taker or risk averse, people person or analyst, young or old, male or female, broke or with funds. The entrepreneur world is full of diversity and opportunity.

You do need a clear goal backed by passion and determination, and these are helped by knowing what type of entrepreneur you are.

Few new entrepreneurs really know their own goals and to prosper in business that is an essential starting point. It might be a simple goal, usually it is more complex. Everyone says they want to make money, but actually a lot don't, and those that do have some very different motivations for doing so. You need to understand these drives in yourself, as they will go a long way to determining your entrepreneur profile.

How do you get started?

Over the years after talking to many budding and existing entrepreneurs I have come to realize that the word 'entrepreneur' is just too general. Stop ten people in the street, ask them what the word means for them and you will get ten different answers.

The danger is that when someone 'escapes corporate world' they tend to think of the 'start-up' business as their only option. I have identified five classifications of choice (not including corporate and social entrepreneurs) and the start-up business is usually the worst one for them to cut their teeth on. Read on to find out why …

There are five main types of entrepreneur although some are elements of more than one. Understanding these is an essential first step before embarking on any venture.

How you start depends on your motivation. The most common career goal I hear from aspiring entrepreneurs is the ability to control their own destiny. This held true for each of the five categories below. Each category can be started on a part-time or sole trader basis. I emphasize this as many successful, now large enterprises started this way. Those that wanted to get bigger did so in reaction to their market demand, and thus there is an inbuilt safety element and the capital costs are kept to a minimum.

Many entrepreneurs start by working part time while maintaining their main income. Often this can provide a second vocation that could be expanded should redundancy strike, or when a major growth opportunity presents itself. When practical, this choice can provide a safe bridge towards becoming fully independent. Others go for it, putting in all their personal resources. Some raise venture capital. Later in the book I will share with you some alternative sources of raising capital with minimal risk or cost. In this chapter we shall first look at what being an entrepreneur means, followed by a discussion about the five categories. By the end you will be in a position to consider what type of entrepreneur you would like to be.

You can start on your own even part time for most types of enterprise, whatever your ultimate goals are. My research shows that, if practical, this path tends to yield more success than the others, followed by buying a franchise in an established operation. Buying a business is also a safe route, as the business should be profitable already. Starting small is the ideal way to test the market and get lots of live feedback without any major commitment.

You can then risk putting more resources behind your ideas from a situation of growing confidence. I have met many people who have, say, been made redundant or come back from abroad with a capital sum wondering what to do. That dream to run a business though suddenly seems a lot different from the other side of the counter.

What are the key qualities of an entrepreneur?

Someone who can make things happen. Innovation, creativity, risk taking, independence and a strong character are at the heart of entrepreneurship. A person who has decided to take control of their future and become self-employed, usually but not necessarily by creating their own business, product or service. Entrepreneurs thus add value to society by providing what the consumer requires, especially when they change their wants and needs.

Entrepreneurs compete with themselves, always wanting to improve their own performance. They never believe they have reached their potential and know that success or failure lies within their personal control or influence. You will need strength of character without a doubt. I think that it is no coincidence that many of the successful entrepreneurs from any part of the world have or had a strong character and maintained a high standard of honesty, integrity and ethics.

What does it take to become a successful entrepreneur?

What images does the word entrepreneur conjure up in your mind? For most they are attractive ones of adventure, freedom, independence, fast cars, luxury houses, holidays, success, wealth, etc. These are certainly real rewards of success. Like everything worth having though, there are some challenges to overcome along the way.

Hard work, for example, is certainly a common habit of successful entrepreneurs. Yet hard work to be effective has to be the right work. In the early stages of the business you are the most valuable resource. Therefore how you spend your time can be your most important decision. Take a moment and ask yourself this question: 'What is the most valuable work I should be doing this week?'

You need to start thinking like a great entrepreneur. People make the mistake of behaving and even spending like they are already wealthy. This is how they see a successful entrepreneur behaving. However, how the great achievers behaved at the stage you are at now is the key area to model. Here, and usually later, they are extremely thrifty, wanting every penny to work in their business. The secret of real success is not in the eyes of others. Is status important to you? It is important to most people; it is not about the outward image but the internal thinking. True entrepreneurs are not as motivated by external measures such as status and material possessions but more by internal satisfactions. They can become famous from achieving wealth and high living standards but quite often this is a side effect of their motivations.

Being a successful entrepreneur to me is about improving society, adding things that were not there before. I don't think of Bill Gates's wealth in terms of how many billions he has, but in how he has helped me and many millions of others with his software. Similarly I think of Jeff Bezos's (of Amazon) wealth in terms of how I enjoy shopping and looking at books online. When I think of Walt Disney, I'm impressed by all the smiling faces he created! Of course they have all accumulated personal wealth, but if that is your only target you are nothing more than a miser. The wealth of money is nothing compared to the wealth of being totally free to think, create, innovate at will, and the knowledge that you have added value to society. An entrepreneur is an innovator, inspirer, leader, creator who adds to the lives of customers, staff, shareholders and themselves. Their life is full of excitement, energy, fun and friends. From my experience in the recruitment industry it offers more job satisfaction than any other.

The potential rewards though are very high indeed; your potential income and wealth are unlimited. The timescale can also be a great deal shorter to success. It is not an easy path, but with this book it is a much easier one, learning from those who have trodden the path before you, passing back their advice. Once you have started along this path there are only two things that can stop you reaching the end, in my opinion. One is giving up and the second is not learning as you go.

Let us now move on to look at the different types of entrepreneur.

SMILE your way to success

SMILE is my acronym for the five types of entrepreneur. You may be a hybrid of more than one. Knowing your profile is important to maximize your chance of success and happiness.

* *S* is for System, someone who is happy to buy into a proven formula and work it.
* *M* is for Money, for those whose only measure of success is money in the bank (not what you buy with the money).
* *I* is for Innovator, the creative among you who enjoy developing new ideas.
* *L* is for Lifestyle, for those who want to work their hobby.
* *E* is for Empire builders who want power and influence and to see their brand everywhere.

It is important which type you naturally are and which type you want to be, as there may be a difference. Each type has different strengths and weaknesses, each a different path to success (covered in the next chapter) based on a foundation of common principles. In practice you may be a composite of more than one. You smile as an entrepreneur when you know which one you are and focus upon it.

System entrepreneurs

Business is systemic. It is about the working in harmony of a variety of resources, people of different disciplines, level, and locations, equipment, offices, computers, marketing, accounting, etc. They all have to work together and are dependent on each other. Thus when the system is well designed it caters for all needs and is reduced to the simplest formula possible. That way everyone understands what is expected of them. Growth is made easy because the system is just being duplicated, a proven formula grows another tentacle.

The great success of McDonald's is an extremely efficient business model. It operates all of its '30,000 plus' restaurants around the world to the same basic formula. Every process is in the manual. Every situation that might and has arisen is dealt with in exactly the same way everywhere.

So once the original creativity has been innovated and then tweaked for efficiency a business can grow by taking in partners. In the case of McDonald's this is through franchising. One must not tinker with the proven system, nor wish to, as that road leads to failure.

Another example is in network marketing, often called multi-level or referral marketing. A distributor network is established based upon a system that works. So are you prepared, happy even, to work the system that someone else has designed in which you have no say? If you are, then working the system can make you wealthy, there is no doubt of that, as long as you choose a good franchise, network marketing or system to join and that you work it in the way it was designed to be worked. Risk is greatly reduced, there should already be a proven market. Clearly there is no need for creativity, so if this is not one of your skill sets, being a system entrepreneur should appeal.

Money entrepreneurs

Money entrepreneurs are focused on storing as much financial wealth as possible. Their goal is money itself and not the things they will buy with the money. Their goal is high wealth not income level. In the extreme, these people will have no concept that there could be any other objective in running their own business. They tend not to enjoy their work as they will always focus their energies on where most money is, rather than their own passion. They have the advantage of being naturally in touch with the market and they will offer only things that they know will sell well. When they are successful they use their money to make more money taking full advantage of compound interest and leverage principles. They want to become as wealthy as they possibly can.

In less extreme cases they realize that the first goal of any business is to make a profit consistently, otherwise there is no business. They are also prudent enough to store money through a good period as an insurance against a lean period. To some extent we all need to be money entrepreneurs; it is, after all, what makes the world go around. The other advantage in setting your goal as money is that it is very easy to measure. Sales and profit targets are either reached or not. It is thus simple, measurable and must be a prime focus of any enterprise, whatever the other driving passions are.

Innovative entrepreneurs

To many the word 'entrepreneurs' is virtually synonymous to the word 'creative'. After all, a new enterprise does things differently from what has gone before it. A company can even be seen as an art form. Amazon changed the way we bought books. McDonald's changed the way we ate, eBay® changed the way we bought things. Tim Berners Lee, creator of the world wide web, changed the way people all over the world talked to each other.

The joy and challenge of creation becomes entrepreneurial when it meets commercial goals. Art might be beautiful but is there a market for it? When you focus your attention on the needs of people that are not currently being met as well as they could, you have the potential to create something better. Creation gives what business people call a USP – unique selling point. It becomes special, giving an edge over competitors.

Creative people, therefore, become innovative entrepreneurs when they start their focus on potential customers. They create better things, ways of doing things. Does this sound like you?

Lifestyle entrepreneurs

How great would it be for your hobby and passion and your business to be one and the same? When you love every minute of what you do, profit is a bonus, not the point of the enterprise. After all, if you had riches you would just spend all your time on your hobby anyway, so why not short-cut the process? A lifestyle entrepreneur is one whose primary motive is working their hobby.

When you plan to remain small you can cover for each other, work as a close-knit team, and management is relatively straightforward. Once you have a secure client base, profits can be high and the lifestyle can be thoroughly satisfying. You also have a capital asset that you can sell, should you wish to.

Employing staff immediately allows greater efficiencies in terms of delegating specialist tasks. It also means greater responsibilities and staff need managing. You need to make sure that your productivity, while training, managing and motivating, is not compromised. They are not capitalists, they are just selling their labour, and for a monthly bill you have to keep paying. For most, loyalty will be dependent on you paying them, although I have personal experience of members of staff offering to forgo salary when the pressure was on. These are rare, special individuals. Your challenge as an entrepreneur is to ensure that the value they add to the enterprise is more than you are paying them. You have a very strong direct effect on their productivity. You can choose them, train, lead and motivate them to give their best. You have a moral responsibility also for their career. The human race does not exist to be exploited for profit. They are stakeholders in your business, dedicating a large chunk of their life to making it work.

Empire entrepreneurs

Empire entrepreneurs want their brand, their name to be everywhere. Whatever stage they are at they want to be bigger, with a bigger reach, more power and influence. They have no end position, they always want more. Just achieving financial freedom is not enough for them. They love growing and will continue for ever.

Are you the next Bill Gates? Do you want to be? If you had his financial wealth what would you do with it? Your answers will give an insight to your values and motivations. The British army unit the Special Air Service has a motto, 'Who Dares Wins'. This enterprising group achieves things even if they seem impossible. This is the attitude you need to adopt to build a major multinational group (but only use the door when you enter the office!). First, think big, believe that you can, research your plans thoroughly and perfect your formula for making money and how you intend to grow it. How, for example, will you finance such massive growth and in what timescale? There are always options: franchising, venture capital, partnering with a major company. These all need to be worked through to find the most appropriate choice.

You need a vision of the future and to think long term. Rockefeller clearly rose above his competitors by seeing the importance of economies of scale and how they could operate in his industry. Like many great entrepreneurs he was obsessed with efficiency and control of costs. Aspiring entrepreneurs who come to me for advice are focused on sales and marketing. I thus find it interesting that the great successes in business had their focus on the other side of the profit equation.

You can start small and grow in reaction to your market. Michael Marks, for example, started retailing his goods by knocking on doors and standing on street corners. This led to market trading, then a shop, then another shop. You may have been in one of them, they are called Marks & Spencer. His famous phrase 'Don't ask the price, it is a penny', did not come from marketing genius but because he could not speak English when he started. A simple sign on his stall solved any problems, and made life easier for potential customers. Yet this simplicity of pricing existed for a long time in the company, showing how much easier it is to run a business that has simple principles and focus.

The profile test

To an entrepreneur, achievement can mean wealth beyond their wildest dreams. Entrepreneurs, certainly in America which is a relatively young nation and in Europe, form the largest grouping of millionaires. That is why entrepreneurs are prepared to take the risks and, even in their darkest hour, few would want to be an employee again.

When pure 'money entrepreneurs' are successful, they use their money to make more money, taking full advantage of compound interest and leverage principles. People who win the lottery invariably are not happy, it is just not enough. Entrepreneurship can give you satisfaction on a whole range of levels.

Look at the five types of entrepreneur (SMILE). How much does each type appeal to you? Mark them out of ten, where 10 = appeals most and 1 = appeals least. Finally, list them in order of priority.

Now, what about risk? Well for me, I have been there and done it before, so the risk associated with start-up is very much less than for a novice. I also have a strong sales background which helps for this type of enterprise.

If, like me, Innovator is highest or high you will be happier in situations where you can apply your own ideas. Start-ups are an obvious choice, whereas franchises and network marketing opportunities should be avoided.

If Money is your top choice you could well be the opposite of the above as risk is greatly reduced and you are working a proven formula designed to build wealth.

Lifestyle at or near the top might mean you want to work your hobby or be a self-employed consultant. Limited potential for profits but if you can make ends meet and do what you love, you have a formula for happiness.

Empire builders should go for start-ups, network marketing or buy an existing business with a brand that gives it the potential for growth. The latter two are far less risky but the first offers a complete blank sheet to express ideas.

At the next level, analysis depends more on specific circumstances, for example if you are interested in health and beauty products, tired of being short of cash and wanting the good life, the four more or less equal top for you are Money, System, Lifestyle and Empire. Then an established network marketing business distributing health products could be ideal for you.

When you know your profile you need to assess the profile of each opportunity and see quite simply if it matches yours.

_3_

_entry
routes_

What types of opportunities are best matched to your profile? Many business people talk about action being the most important thing. However, I say that action in the wrong direction will lead you into problems rather quickly. First make sure you are on the right path and then take lots of action. This chapter is all about looking at the most appropriate business opportunities open to you and making an intelligent choice according to your personal goals, talents and personality profile and passion.

When you have made your choice, design an action plan. Make it one that increases your current income. Avoid one that involves loans, overdrafts or putting your house on the line. Contrary to popular belief entrepreneurs can be as much risk avoiders as takers. So make part of your plan full of, 'What would I do ifs'. Move fast but thoroughly through this stage. When that is done you need to find specific money-making opportunities.

Once you know your entrepreneur profile type you are in a position to recognize what type of opportunity will be the best and most appropriate one for you.

In this chapter we look at how to give you your Street SMARTS which is my acronym for the six main groupings of opportunity.

* **S** is for Self-employment
* **M** is for Multi-level marketing
* **A** is for Acquire a business
* **R** is for Royalty
* **T** is for Turnkey operations
* **S** is for Start-up

Let us look at them each in turn.

Self-employment

Your career and perhaps your out-of-work activities have made you an expert in something. You hear about people with whom you identify, with how much they invoice per day, and you think: 'That could be me'. There are no real set-up costs and already you have an address book full of contacts.

So you make the move. You are self-employed, independent, your own boss doing what you want. You are free to follow your dream. The sky is now the limit.

Well, perhaps. The dream can turn to a nightmare if you do not follow some basic principles of business. Profit must be your first motive, not doing what you want to do or even helping others. If you do not consistently make a profit you won't survive.

You eagerly prepare what you want to offer (materials, website, business cards, newsletter, blogs, etc.) until you are proud of all of them. Then when everything is ready you go into selling mode: network, advertise, canvass, call prospective clients, attend events, etc.

If you want to make money this is not the best approach. Do it the other way around. Forget the website, well-designed business card, newsletter, at least for now. Invest nothing apart from your time. Instead talk to people generally about what you can offer and ask lots of questions, and listen to the answers. Do it with an open mind, assume nothing, and don't filter out what you don't want to hear. When six out of ten people tell you about something that is a problem for them then you have a market need. When one person tells you they have something bothering them now, you have a sale. If you can package something together that will solve their problem then you have a long-term profitable business. A business that won't need a lot of selling, because it relies on listening. When you have done this, design a website and business cards focusing on how you solved this specific problem. Design it for your potential market to be impressed and served.

You are ready to start a business when you have the answer to the following question: 'Who currently desires something that is currently unfulfilled in the general area that I offer skills?'

And when you have the answer, ask: 'How can I serve more people for less work at a better price?'

The next mistake often made by the self-employed is not really knowing their own skill set, and thus not selling in the area that gives them greatest potential. I meet all the time:

* NLP practitioners who suffer phobias
* sales trainers who have not got a strong portfolio of clients
* telesales course providers who mailshot their courses
* financial advisers who are broke
* relationship experts who are desperately lonely and single.

What qualifies you to be a consultant to others? What are your credentials? What are your successes and talents? These questions are different from: What are you most interested in doing? If I buy services from someone, I want them to be successful in this area not just knowledgeable and certainly not experienced through failure alone. UNLESS they have overcome it.

The next huge mistake is thinking that you have your own business with great potential because you are a freelance independent consultant. From a financial/business point of view you are actually in no better a situation than your employed counterparts. You are also now personally responsible for everything.

Your financial formula is simple and much the same as an employee. What it boils down to is selling yourself for an hourly rate. You can increase that hourly rate or the number of hours you work in the week, but both have limited scope. No leverage. No money when you sleep. No passive, residual income.

In fact the self-employed consultant can be worse off. Their employed counterpart has all sorts of support available to them: secretaries, IT experts, a sales and marketing department, bookkeeping, web design; all sorted. The self-employed consultant thinks they can fee earn 20 days a month. They soon realize that marketing, attending courses, having the flu, administration, preparation, etc., are all unpaid activities that burn up a lot of time.

You need to think differently and stop being like a little mouse going around and around on a treadmill in your cage.

If your target is to be the leading expert in your niche, do the following: produce materials that can be sold with no extra input from yourself. Then employ someone to do all support tasks previously mentioned. If you can invoice anywhere between £100 and £2,500 per day for your services then employing someone part or full time will make you more profitable. Analyse everything you do in the week by the hour and put a value on it. Bookkeeping can be done for £x per hour, admin for ..., etc. If you are not at your top rate, farm it out. Experts like accountants, and website designers are also cheaper. Because they take a fifth of the time you would, to do the tasks, and get it right a lot more often. Don't be shy to increase costs to buy yourself more time. Get going first and use that initial money to jump to the next step.

If you want to get rich this way there are two choices: you need a formidable day rate, most of which you then invest wisely against a rainy day. Or you need materials that have got a clear market AND you have found a means to tap into that market. Produce, for example, an audio clip for internet download, webcast, teleclass, DVD, video, CD-ROM, book, board game on how you do what you do. But make sure you have a route to your market first. The best ways are the ones that are free. There are so many of those that I would not look further. Anyone with a website dealing in your area is a prospect so ask to put clear adverts on their site for a sales commission. Amazon will put your book (audio or written) on their site. So will thousands of other web masters. This is all potential passive income and all free advertising which does not continually drain your resources.

In summary, there are six ways you can make a good financial return as a self-employed consultant:

1 Consistently secure very high billings and invest the bulk of it.
2 Produce products, sold through others, that can give you a long-term residual income.
3 Build a business, not dependent on you, that can be sold.
4 Market a patented system for other self-employed people in your field to follow.
5 A mixture of the above.
6 Inherit a fortune or win the lottery while you are working!

Loneliness is another potential pitfall. You have no one to bounce ideas off. Being your own boss for many people makes them realize just how much they were dependent on their boss for motivation, stick or carrot. No one is watching over you.

The self-employed are often fearful of selling. There is no boss now to make them do it. If you have something good, believe in what you offer. Then all you have to do is go around asking how you can help people. Focus on solving their problems. If you focus on helping others instead of yourself you will find deals come to you. It will also take your mind naturally into a healthy market research mode. You will come across as genuine and professional.

Self-employment, or starting something while you are still in full-time employment, can be a good first step as an entrepreneur. We will be covering some such options later. You have broken the corporate chains and you are your own boss. You are still at this stage though dependent on earned income from your own labour. To become rich and secure you really need to earn from things other than your labour. If you are ill for two weeks or take a holiday the business is closed. You are limited by the highest rate you can charge and the maximum number of hours you can work.

This, however, might be the lifestyle you want. You are your own boss, you do not have the responsibility of others, and you can be creative in your own way.

At this level greater efficiency can be made by delegating as much as possible. For example, employ a part-time bookkeeper on an hourly rate to do your accounting. The cost should be a lot less than your charge-out rate. Everything you do you must cost by the hour. Anything that is less than your charge-out rate is a contender for subcontracting.

If you wish to progress as a business you need to do at least one of two things:

1 Make products relative to your expertise for sale.
2 Expand, which usually means taking on staff. The advantage is that you can wait until you are overwhelmed with work then grow from a position of strength and security.

Multi-level marketing

Multi-level marketing, sometimes known as network or referral marketing, is a potentially great way to run your own business with many substantial benefits. Although it does not suit most people, it might be right for you. The idea is that you sign up for a distributorship with a network marketing company. Then you have the right to buy their products as a wholesaler and the right to sell them on without having to fund the cost. Therefore, you can consume and you can sell and receive the commissions. You can sell on two bases: retail, which is straightforward, or you can introduce somebody to the business so that they become a distributor. Bear in mind that, as there are no retail outlets and many of the costs associated with a traditional business, the distributors share the higher profit margins.

As you introduce more people and the people you bring in do the same, over time you should have a self-developing network. Say, for example, you introduce three people. Then those people introduce three people each. Then those nine people introduce three people each. Then those 27 people introduce three people each.

Then those 81 people introduce three people each. Your income is a percentage of the total sales coming from your group. This rate gets higher as your network grows bigger. Therefore you can grow your network only by helping those in your network to grow theirs. Those who introduced you have a responsibility and an interest in supporting you in every way. As everyone's income is determined by what they initiated, everyone joins on the same level.

Good organizations don't commit you to a minimum purchase level and have regular training support from leaders. The advantages are that you need no real capital to start off and you can start while still in full-time work. You are operating a proven system that works. When you have a network you have a passive income, even if you take a holiday. The success of network marketing is staggering and has created a large number of self-employed millionaires.

Often people work as a couple, sharing the duties where they are best suited. It really is a system where you get out in direct proportion to what you put in, and couples can push, encourage and support each other. It does not happen over night; it is certainly not for someone looking to 'get rich quick'. Initially, like any entrepreneurial opportunity, it means investing long hours upfront for financial freedom in the future. The rewards do not come short term, like in an employee opportunity.

Those who do not stay the distance and drop out tend to bad mouth the company. Understandably who is going to say it was them rather than the system that failed? You have to be prepared to take rejection as most people to whom you offer the business opportunity will not join, or worse join half heartedly then drop out when they realize it is a long haul. People sometimes get over keen on persuading others to join their network, which becomes irritating. Most successful people in this category who I have met clearly have high standards of honesty, integrity and leadership. There is no disputing, though, the thousands of people who have become millionaires through network marketing. In the USA, which produces a lot of statistics, each year's new crop of millionaires include more than one in five who achieved it through network marketing. It is worth considering as it involves only a token investment and can be started part time from home.

As someone who has been employed in sales, I know that companies for which I worked 20 years ago are still milking clients who I brought to them. In network marketing you earn permanently on anything that you develop.

To succeed at it you have to be more focused on helping other people succeed, to succeed yourself. It is not about creativity, it is about duplicating a proven system. If you want to be independent and become financially free but do not have a creative idea or capital to invest, it is certainly worth looking at. Apart from your time there is also no risk of capital loss. There are many companies to choose from and their names appear in many business listings. As most people join on a personal introduction (they prefer to give their advertising budget to distributors), one can wait a long time before someone prospects you. Try surfing the net and pick a product/service that interests you, that you believe in and that you therefore wish to promote.

Acquire a business

You could buy and then improve an existing business. This can be done through a management buy out (MBO) from inside, or buy in (MBI) from outside. Or you can just buy a business from the market. Let us look at MBO/MBIs first.

For an MBO/MBI an entrepreneur needs the backing of a financial institution to put them and their team in charge. They see the main asset of any company to be the team who manages it. Even in this technological age it is still people who make the changes. A new team is often successful in a failing business. Often the management has, by definition, bought into the old ways of doing things, which is where their knowledge and expertise lies.

A new team has not bought in to the old ways and sees things from a totally fresh perspective. This seeing things in a different way is right at the heart of entrepreneurial skills. Turnarounds are all about using resources in more opportunistic ways. Often entrepreneurs go in with advantages over the old management. If they are buying in through a financial institution, a strong backer will give them all sorts of advantages. That backing alone will give the team the ability to negotiate far better terms with suppliers. Debts on the company are now far more secure and, with backing, growth is a real possibility. Therefore, both price, in the anticipation of bigger orders in the future, and terms of credit can be made on more favourable terms. There are plenty of examples of companies being turned around by doing just that.

If you have expertise in an industry and a loyal team, then an MBI could be a viable option for you. Simply, you find a financial backer to buy a company and put your team in to manage it. Often venture capitalists will already have stakes in companies that are not going to plan and putting a fresh management team in is very attractive to them. You have to convince them that you can make substantial improvement where the current team is failing. You may even spot one or more companies in your industry that you can form into a group under your management.

If you have a pedigree in an industry and a convincing strategy, you have an opportunity to avoid the high risks of a start-up and concentrate on an organization that is already up and running. Many businesses have had dramatic turnarounds when a new management was put in place. Individuals like Lee Iacoca (Chrysler) and John Harvey Jones (ICI) have both made dramatic changes to the companies they led when they were given the helm. This reinforces my view and certainly the one taken by venture capitalists that any company's greatest asset is its management team.

Buying a business has many advantages. First, it is far easier to raise finance because there is a track record and profits to offer. Second, as already said, it can be bought with the help of owner financing or by factoring the company's own invoices. Often you can pick a business where you immediately add value through your contacts, expertise or other assets. Getting a company to increase profits is a hundred times easier than getting a start-up to break even. As valuations of small businesses are based on a multiple of profits, you can literally increase market value every day. Risks are clearly far less when acquiring an already profitable business.

Royalty

In this category of entrepreneur I include people who are not necessarily running companies at all. They are included because of their personal enterprise in creating something new that has a commercial potential. They have the potential to make a substantial passive income source. In fact, many inventors go on to run companies, but this is not essential.

This category obviously includes me as the author of this book. I also produce audio books. All of these products are produced, marketed and sold for me by someone else. My risks and investment are minimal, apart from my time, and the potential income from royalties and spin-offs such as talks, training and consultancy can be substantial. You can do the same for whatever you do and produce any number of information products on your expertise.

Alternatively, you may be a potential inventor, working on an item that will do something really special and be in demand. James Dyson developed a wheelbarrow with a ball instead of a wheel. He then went on to develop a new system for a vacuum cleaner. His challenging of the existing ways of doing things is an inspiration to us all. If this is the sort of entrepreneur who inspires and motivates you, the thing you need to know most about are patents. However, in a global world don't rely wholly on this protection. Suing someone who breaks your patent, or gets near to it can be very costly in time and money: two resources of which you will have a very limited supply. Besides, until you have a large established market no one will probably notice or be interested.

Consider not just who your invention would benefit but who it would threaten. Does it render an existing product obsolete? If so, the current manufacturers are most definitely threatened.

They will have a lot of power to protect their interests. Having the law on your side may not prove to be that beneficial if you have to finance a long drawn out legal battle conducted in several countries.

One option, of course, is to take your invention to that big company in exchange for a royalty deal. If you cannot beat them join them. They have resources for finance, marketing, development, testing, etc.

Turnkey operations

A turnkey operation is where you buy a business system from somebody which is prepared, tried, tested and proven, and ready to go. You just have to turn the key to get it going. The most common type is a franchise that means buying an operating unit from a company and paying an ongoing management fee. The advantages are that you are buying something that is proven, tested, has a workable system for every process and, of course, you are not alone.

The modern day form of franchising, called the 'business format franchise', was really started by Ray Kroc when he decided that this was the best way to develop his McDonald's restaurant. Six thousand units later, when he became the world's largest restaurant business, nobody could doubt the success of the franchising formula. There are now well over five times that number of units. As each franchisee finances their own business it allows the growth of a substantial number of outlets. There are now many franchises available, from high street shops to management consultancies.

If you have a capital sum to invest, a franchise greatly reduces your risk and bypasses many of the problems start-up entrepreneurs have in more traditional businesses. Every problem has already been looked at/occurred in a franchise and there are full support services available. Typically, franchisors make their money by charging a percentage of sales for their support, branding, marketing, etc., and when there are products involved they can also control and supply the product. The strength of a franchise is its proven system. It is, put simply, a formula for making money where all you have to do is turn the key and run the operation.

Any business is a risk, although increasingly people find their jobs to be insecure and are thus more likely to make the leap, as the risk perception divide narrows. In a job, however well paid, you have no leverage. You will always be limited to what boils down to your own labour.

The business format franchise really started in the UK with pubs, then car dealerships. Then came a plethora of fast-food chains starting with the most famous McDonald's. Ever envied the daily cash receipts of your local McDonald's? Don't be naïve though; even with McDonald's you cannot sit back and just expect it all to happen. This is often the failing of franchisees who expect to sit back, employ someone and just receive the profits. All businesses have to be worked and grown. Even McDonald's a few years ago put in its first loss in history. Many franchisors have told me that their biggest headache is that people may have the cash and interest, but this does not mean that they have the skills or even the motivation necessary to make it work. Like all entrepreneurs they have to take responsibility to make their success.

A turnkey operation is clearly for the System entrepreneur types who have some money to invest. For further information on franchising, see the companion volume in this series, *Get Started in Franchising* (Hodder Education, 2010).

Start-ups

Start-ups are the hardest form of entrepreneurship. Obvious if you think about it. The business products/services are new, there are no established customers, there is no proof that anyone will buy, the business model is unproven, the management team or person is inexperienced. There are no repeat orders or loyal customers. Even with first sales, reaching breakeven can take a number of years. The entrepreneurs have to somehow finance their own living and try to avoid draining precious resources from the business. All of this means that the pressure while doing this is immense and growing. People around you will cast doubt, and you will cast doubt on yourself. If capital gain is your main goal then buying a business is far quicker and far safer, with a far more certain, far easier to finance, end result.

However, the world's richest people are those who followed the start-up route. Their names and companies are all around us. The two people who started eBay® became billionaires before ten years had elapsed. The Google™ entrepreneurs achieved billionaire status in nearer five years. Bill Gates, of course, is the richest man in the world. All of these people individually have more wealth than the combined England football squad and the top ten selling rock stars!

So we are talking of very high risk with the highest possible pay off. In addition to this the entrepreneur has complete freedom to be creative. So start-up is the option if your profile is strongly I and M, less of L (SMILE!) and perhaps some E!

Tea for two or three

Whatever business opportunity you go for you may consider doing it with a partner(s).

There are many advantages to partnership, not being alone being a major one. There are, however, some ground rules. I have found that when partners are not equal, even for good reason, sooner or later this will lead to conflict. Issues around unequal contributions should be balanced in some other way, keeping share holdings equal. Perhaps on first drawings from profits, or a debt to the company from the less contributing partner. This money value can then be equalized by one of the partners drawing less for a while, for example. There are many easy and practical formulas; this is one of the advantages. Another is that your reports and accounts are private and can remain confidential to the partners. A disadvantage is that you are liable personally for any debts of the enterprise and liable for any actions any partner makes.

Everyone will want their ideas put forward. The strength of the partnership should be in all the partners having ideas. If one of the partners considers their ideas as leading and better than the others, conflict will again arise. The partners have to have the same objective for the business. If one, for example, is motivated purely by profit and another by achieving excellence and leadership in a product line, then at some point the objectives will be divergent not convergent. Again conflict arises.

If you want a lifestyle business then you want to keep the whole equity. If profit is your main motive then your interest will be maximizing the value of your shareholdings in the future. The partnership formula in itself does not suggest you even maintain a majority.

Would you prefer to keep 100% of all your researched ideas? Or 30% with an experienced partner and £500,000 of venture capital in the bank. The point being with the financial head start that 30% is likely to be worth more in five years than the 100%.

Exit routes

By this point you should know the type of entrepreneur you are and what entrepreneurial opportunity classification is most suitable for you. Give some thought now to where you want to end up.

If you have a lifestyle business you will probably want to do that for ever. If money is your main goal then your best bet is probably to sell for capital gain. Current UK tax laws favour this route and it gives you a chance to not have your eggs in one basket. You can re-invest three quarters of sales proceeds and start a new business with the remaining quarter. If you are an E in SMILE, buying other businesses will probably be the faster, most attractive route for you. Franchises often grow by buying more franchises in the system in which they have already proven their success.

If you have invested in multi-level marketing then you can stop at any time and enjoy the ongoing passive income. You now have time freedom which can be invested in other activities, business or personal.

Protecting the downside

Always look to reduce risk, especially on a first venture. Think about what may go wrong and have a contingency plan in place. This may sound negative; it is in fact realistic and practical.

Risks can be reduced in all sorts of ways:

1 Identify and verify a clear market need that is not being satisfied.
2 Start something that does not require capital or putting your signature to large sums.
3 Join a club (like my 100K Club) and surround yourself by people who can give you free, unbiased advice.
4 Keep to a business that you know something about or expect to learn.
5 Test the market before you go into production.
6 Get pre-orders and deposits before you start.
7 Join an existing business as an independent agent.
8 Pick something that everyone needs and repeat orders.

To help entrepreneurs reduce the financial risk, without restricting the upside, I setup the 100K Club. As part of our risk-reducing support for new ventures:

* We have set up self-employment opportunities that require no money investment in safe order industries. For example, we offer Associate positions with Crane Office Supplies, and provide full support services with no investment.
* We offer Venture Capital raising and will test and improve your business plan and support you in your negotiations.
* We show you that you can get cash up front, in order to avoid debt or giving out equity.
* We teach you how to use social media facilities, such as LinkedIn and Ecademy, to promote your business for free.

There are lots of ways to protect the downside – take this aspect of entrepreneurship seriously.

4

seeing opportunities

In the last week you have walked past at least a dozen opportunities. Did you see them? Reflect back and think. How many can you now spot?

You need to develop your opportunity spectacles and when you do you will notice that there is abundance not shortage. The trick is focusing on just the one that suits your business goals.

We live in an unprecedented time in history of not only rapid but accelerating change. New innovations in business today can be outdated even within a year. This means in your particular market place you need to have the vision to put all the pieces together and position yourself to where things are moving. This makes sure you are in the right place at the right time doing the right thing. Always remember people buy things that they want and have a benefit to them. Firstly do that and then build a business model that supplies those needs profitably.

What shall I do?

The question 'What do I want to do?' must be adapted to 'What do people want to buy?' I see businesses on- and offline opening all the time which clearly have no market. You may live in Oxford and dream of owning your own yachting supplies shop, but do you have a local market? Work is ultimately about doing something for somebody else. The real trick is to marry what people need to what you have a passion for and capability of supplying. Remember that if you start by finding a market, then selling will be relatively easy.

You can become self-employed, take on a franchise, buy a business, become a corporate entrepreneur, invent a new device or launch something new with the intention of making it a major multinational. Opportunity spotting is not just about getting an initial idea, it is a way of life. It covers every aspect and process of your business, all the time. Even after you have just improved a process, you should immediately start looking for opportunities to improve it further, never being satisfied with performance. We will now explore some of these options so you can decide which one is for you.

Here are a few examples of where you may look for opportunities:

* a new product or service
* enhance an existing product
* a new market for an existing product
* a new application for an existing product
* better arrangements with suppliers
* better promotion, advertising
* improve efficiency and speed of ordering
* new contact sources
* applications of new technology
* new and better ways of doing anything
* whenever you hear people frustrated at something not being available
* ways to leverage your current resources.

Acting on inspiration

Have you ever travelled abroad and had the following interesting experiences?

1 Noticing something in that country which you consider better than at home and you cannot imagine why it does not exist where you live?

2 Noticing something that is worse in the country visited than at home and wondered why they do not do it your way?

3 Noticing something quite different and cannot figure out if it is better or worse than at home, but it has given you ideas?

That is the entrepreneur in you trying to come out.

This is how entrepreneurs think: they first observe, analyse and constantly ask themselves questions like the above. They keep asking 'Why?' questions. It is easy to get it wrong, but that gives you valuable information to help you get it right next time. In addition, when you get it right, the payoffs are truly exciting. Actually the process of being an entrepreneur is an exciting adventure in itself. Is your work at the moment an exciting adventure? It should be.

You need to maximize the use of resources, relating this all the time to potential sales and profit. Look around you: what is there that could be used in a different way to more effect? What resources can you see that are being underemployed? What needs are being frustrated? What technological, cultural, sociological or other changes are going to create new needs? This is why entrepreneurs start turning their garages and spare room into a cheap and convenient office.

The opportunist

Non-entrepreneurs think that we find an idea then run with it. In reality, you need to be constantly looking for new opportunities and constantly updating your original one. Ideas in themselves are ten a penny; the real game is to turn ideas into commercial reality and not just talk. Entrepreneurs are not in the business of saying,

'I told you somebody would invent a product that would do that.' You have to make things happen through your belief, conviction, determination, enthusiasm, commitment and a practical ability.

The five steps to spot opportunities:

1 Ask these magic questions:
   a What or whom has presented a potential opportunity to me today?
   b From the people who I met today, what need do they seem to have?
   c What have I kept hearing from people over the last week?
   d What is happening out there right now? What does this mean there is an increased need for?
   e What do you think people would buy in great numbers if it existed now?
   f What service or product would you buy today if it existed?
2 Read the magic questions at the start of the day, print out a copy and stick it on your wall.
3 Observe and listen as you go through the day.
4 Wait. The questions are in your unconscious working away. You have trained your mind to focus automatically on opportunities. Soon ideas will start flowing. Soon you will realize that commercial opportunities are presented in front of your nose on a daily basis. It is just that they have been invisible to you, and others, before.
5 Never stop looking for those opportunities.

The four steps to turn opportunities into profit:

1 Establish a market price and how to reach it.
2 Determine how much it would cost to produce an initial stock of the product or deliver the service.
3 Work out the finances.
4 Remember to think big but get some feedback first with limited risk. All results are valuable feedback, keep listening.

Your lucky day?

Opportunities come in many shapes and sizes, and they keep coming. They are like trains leaving a mainline station: if you miss one there will be another one leaving at some point. Who knows, it may even be missing a train that puts a once in a lifetime opportunity in front of you. While having an unplanned coffee, you may notice something interesting about the people in the café. Something that you realize would be really useful to them while waiting for a train. Alternatively, perhaps you get talking to someone at the same table and the conversation triggers an idea, or maybe both of you together can offer something that you could not offer alone. Many partnerships have been built this way. It makes me wonder what opportunity will come your way tomorrow. More importantly, will you recognize it and grasp it with both hands?

Ray Kroc on his rounds selling his restaurant equipment called one day on the McDonald brothers' little place. Now, if he was focused just on how much commission he could get selling to this one burger bar, where would he have been today? I wonder how many times you have been on a visit like that and missed the potential that you could have seen. He knew how to ask himself the right questions.

When John D Rockefeller was in the oil business he saw the massive advantages that size brought in terms of negotiating railroad freight rates. Therefore, he focused on joining together many small operators to gain a monopolistic position.

What in your industry is outdated? What is happening that everybody takes for granted, but in fact it no longer has a use? Companies are very quick to make people redundant. They are less quick to make things, processes, or ways of doing things redundant, particularly if the management team's power base is their knowledge and experience of doing it in that old redundant way. That is the opportunity ground for entrepreneurs to enter and update things.

So many firms have resisted the onset of the internet and telecommunications revolution. Older managers are suddenly threatened by a redundant knowledge whilst twenty-somethings are becoming billionaires in their industry. Turning a large company around can be like turning a supertanker around in a harbour. The entrepreneur can move quicker and is not hampered by old outdated ways of doing things, or outdated people resisting change.

In a changing world, the consumer will be looking for new things all the time. Needs change, they are not constant, things go in and out of fashion.

How entrepreneurs make their own luck:

* They look and listen for opportunities constantly.
* They believe that in everything that happens there is opportunity somewhere.
* They think ahead and plan for every contingency.
* They get in tune with what people would pay money for. They then make this their focus.

Certainly there is something in being in the right place at the right time. There are still many parts of the world where being an entrepreneur is frowned upon or even illegal. However, it is human enterprise that creates everything around us. It is the entrepreneurial tradition that made and continues to maintain the USA as the richest country in the world with more than 25% of the planet's wealth and less than 5% of the population.

Failure and other opportunities

You need to have the ability to learn from failure, both your own failure and, more importantly, that of others. It is a lot less uncomfortable to learn from others' mistakes! I really recommend this route first. Information and opportunities are coming at us from all directions non-stop. The trick is to delete the vast majority of it that does not hold opportunity, so that we can see clearly what is left. As Richard Lowden of Green Motion Car Rental says, 'Every time I receive a setback, I immediately ask myself "How can I turn this to my advantage?" All others do is focus on solving the immediate problem.'

Often a failure can be the inspiration for a new launch. Sometimes that failure can be the rejection of an idea you have and your employer rejects. The idea fails before it is given a chance.

I wonder how many ideas are rejected every day by companies that would have turned out to have been great successes. I am yet to meet a venture capitalist who does not tell me about ideas that they rejected which others took on board and which became a great success. I have yet to read a biography of an entrepreneur or an inventor whose ideas did not meet rejection and failure. Their real skill was in finding ways to make their ideas work commercially.

Entreployee

You must be prepared to get out of the 'salary mentality' and sacrifice the short term for a considerably better long term. Many new entrepreneurs compare how they are doing to their previous salary. Understandable, but it has no relevance, and takes your thinking away from a useful productive focus. You will need patience and belief in yourself to keep going.

Here is my impression of an employee over eight weeks.

$$work \rightarrow salary \rightarrow work \rightarrow salary$$

Here it is again, a bit closer to reality.

$$bad\ month \rightarrow salary \rightarrow good\ month \rightarrow same\ salary$$

A job is a business with one client, with no scope to expand, where any capital gain or goodwill you develop is for the profit of that client. If you do well in the year you could earn 20% more in year two and that would be an exceptional success. An entrepreneur looks for leverage of 200% in his first year. Therefore, you have to think bigger. Many prospective entrepreneurs just watch others succeed, fear and the lack of an idea stops them from starting.

Why do you want to be a very successful entrepreneur? People who have been employees for a long time have got used to being motivated by their need for status. Company cars, size of office, pile on carpet, salary grade, executive washrooms, car parking, are graded by status. Entrepreneurs on the other hand will lead a company and muck in with everybody. They roll up their sleeves. This is not just a common expression; entrepreneurs think of their business as their baby and take full pride in every aspect, they will do any task that needs doing. Michael Marks, for example, if he noticed a mess in one of the Marks & Spencer stores, would clear it up himself.

The jump from employee to entrepreneur can be hard, but is a jump worth making. So many venture capitalists' and business angels' networks are inundated by would-be entrepreneurs. Their business plan seems to focus on them receiving a good secure salary. Investors want to invest in a business not pay you. Change focus to business profit not your salary.

If you have been an employee for some time, you have got very used to receiving a salary at the end of each month for your labour. As an entrepreneur it does not work like that. Your thinking has got to change. You are now with the big boys and girls. At some point you have got to come to terms with this. Entrepreneurs are not focused on their salary, they are focusing on wealth building. Entrepreneurs are arguably successful when the enterprise is no longer dependent on them. They have a business and not just self-employment.

Employee thinking	Entrepreneur thinking
I need a monthly salary	I need to make a profit
I need a good pension scheme	I need a capital gain to retire on
I want a promotion	If you want to get to the top, start there
Thank God it's Friday	God, it's Friday already
If I qualify I can get a good job	If I set up my own business I can employ well-qualified people
I want a better job	I have a dream!
What do you want me to do?	What needs doing?
I have a great idea	Here is my new product
I need a secure job	I want to be financially free
I look forward to retiring at 65	I never want to retire, but I will be able to soon
High status	Control own destiny
Keeping on the boss's good side	Independence
Keeping to my strength area	Creativity and variety
Frustration	Incredible job satisfaction
Fixed income	Unlimited income
A higher salary	Capital gain
I have done my best	Never give up

Where do I start?

You start by asking questions and then more questions. Questions get answers, so make sure that yours are well chosen.

'Why' questions, like:

* Why does it happen like this?
* Why can I not get what I want?
* Why do people tolerate this?
* Why has nobody improved this?

'What' questions, like:

* What assumptions are applicable here?
* What was once useful but is now redundant?
* What has changed recently?
* What is redundant here?

'How' questions, like:

* How can I improve this?
* How could it be done better?
* How would I have done this?
* How can I profit from this right now?

'When' questions, like:

* When does this not work well?
* When is the market for this ideal?
* When was this process established?
* When will this idea be outdated?

There are many ways of taking a product and, by giving it a twist, turning it into a moneymaker.

The buck stops here

You are the boss. Everything is your responsibility, even if it is someone else's fault. Remember, winners take responsibility, losers take the blame. So pick your staff, suppliers, premises, marketing, etc. carefully. Take responsibility. This does not mean you have to be an expert on everything or indeed anything. You can employ experts. If you don't want to be the boss you can employ someone who has more experience at it than you. This depends on what type of entrepreneur you have decided to be. The creative entrepreneur often inspires leadership but when it comes to day-to-day management they would sooner delegate. They find it boring and mundane. Be careful of taking on partners though, they will all want to dominate and you will have too many chiefs.

Pennies from heaven

Successful entrepreneurs, of any type, contrary to popular belief, live frugally wanting to invest every penny in their business. They now control their lives, they have made a decision to determine their own destiny. They don't need material, external consumer products to give them status or to make them feel good. They are already free and getting freer. Even when an entrepreneur has made significant wealth, statistics show that the wealthiest people in the country are not the highest spenders. Old habits die hard and wealthy entrepreneurs are surprisingly unlikely to run out to buy flash cars and houses, even now that they can pay cash. If they buy a big house it is probably to use a fair part of it as a cheap office. The house they do buy is also unlikely to be as big as the house they could have bought.

Entrepreneurs will have credit cards but they will use them quite differently. They don't focus on treats and rewards but use them as an easily accessible form of investment, usually for a short-term purpose due to the interest rate.

Therefore, if you have been in that routine for a while, the danger is that your natural entrepreneurial instincts have been eroded. Your natural instincts are to get things you want by making money to pay for them. That way reward and pressure is directly related to real success or failure. This system programmes you to avoid failure and seek more reward, and to do this you make more money. So if you want to be an entrepreneur, harden up and give up an instant satisfaction lifestyle. If that means you go hungry, then go hungry; in practice you won't, that is the whole point. Your unconscious, always seeking to protect you, will focus on taking positive action. You need to get in the habit of short-term pressure, long-term gratification.

Transformations

Large companies have a whole load of specialist departments, big budgets and a range of resources. The entrepreneur has to source things without access to experts, dedicated staff and such resources. As an entrepreneur you have to make it happen yourself, often until you are big enough to enjoy those benefits yourself. If a start-up entrepreneur wants to run a training programme for his six members of staff he probably won't have a training room, flip chart and budget. In addition, if he trains in the day the 'shop' is closed for business. These sorts of practical day-to-day challenges have to be met by thinking on your feet. An entrepreneur would typically network to find a trainer from whom he can pull in a favour, find someone who has a room that they are not using and ask around to borrow a flip chart.

We can have and be heroes

To me, the greatest entrepreneur of all time has to be Walt Disney. (Typical choice of an 'I' in SMILE, you rightly say; the Ms would have gone for Bill Gates!) Hidden behind this viewpoint, of course, is my definition of entrepreneur: creativity, adding value to society, fun, freedom for the mind to wander. Walt's drive did not come from the potential of making big money; that was a side effect that took a long time coming.

Other entrepreneurs were motivated by many different things. What they had in common is that they had a passion for what they wanted at an obsessional level. They mostly took some very big knocks along the way, even going bankrupt sometimes more than once before eventually being successful. Imagine, after going bust twice, having the confidence and belief for your third attempt! Entrepreneurs need a great reservoir of inner strength.

I have asked the question to many people I have coached, 'Who are your three favourite entrepreneurs?' Their answers give away what type of entrepreneur they want to be.

Joining the club

Having run recruitment businesses, I have been approached by venture capitalists to help find board level executives for their ventures. This is a good source of entrepreneurial opportunity that many aspiring entrepreneurs do not think of. These opportunities usually have a big chunk of equity with them.

When someone can do something exceptionally well, it is usually easy for them. This tends to mean that they underestimate the value of that talent. The question, therefore, is to ask yourself and others: 'What is my outstanding talent?' Then ask: 'Who would have a use for that talent?' We need to work to our strengths. If you need other skills employ them, or contract them out. Too many books on entrepreneurship cover all the areas of accounting, marketing, personnel, etc. If you try to learn everything you need to know you will explode. Do what you are good at, recognize what you are not good at and what is needed, and bring it in or contract it out. Even when small, business is still a team sport.

Action stations

You must know where most of your revenue is coming from and focus your attention there. Once started you must build an organization that can exploit effectively the opportunity you spotted. You need the ability to see a market trend and act on it, to attract its money towards you.

Money magnet questions:

* Now what?
* Is my idea good?
* Is it original?
* Is it worth anything?
* Will it sell?
* What is nearest to money?
* What is most lucrative long term?
* What is most lucrative short term?
* What will people pay for?

* What do people not only want but need?
* What would my favourite entrepreneur do if he or she was me?

Entrepreneurship is a practical action-taking endeavour. I think this is a reason why so many successful entrepreneurs had poor school and academic records. Their practical action nature would get too frustrated and not see the point. They are actually highly intelligent but with a different learning style that does not fit in with the school way. Opportunities have to be grasped quickly. The fast usually beat the clever in the entrepreneur game. Have both and you really have an edge. A competitive nature is also a common trait and sport seems to be something they would be more interested in.

Everything that you have done in your life so far has been a necessary path to the incredible destiny that awaits you. Soon you will realize this.

Decision time

Many entrepreneurs have a real talent in getting something created and off the ground. Often, however, this is the point where professional managers need to take over more and more. By recruiting people from quality big company backgrounds you will take on board the processes, procedures and organization that the company increasingly needs. Most entrepreneurs hate this sort of work and want to go on creating. Avoid people from your own industry though, as evidence shows that they will introduce you to the way your larger competitor does it, and to get ahead of it, from your smaller situation, you need to do things better.

So I advise it is important to know what type of entrepreneur you really want to be. As things progress, what role do you see for yourself? I am convinced that people must work where their passion and talent lies to really achieve great things. Don't be dragged into the role of MD if day-to-day management is not your interest. Don't be afraid of appointing somebody over you, who is more experienced in that role. If you are an inventor keep inventing, let somebody else work up the value of your shares.

5

streetwise sales and marketing

Get into a growing market, where competitors are unimpressive. A market that you are in the position to supply easily, ideally where people will search for a path to your door! For every situation there are some tried and tested questions that I have included to get you results fast. These will become an excellent reference resource.

There are many ways that you can effectively market for free. You can even be paid to promote your services as this book is doing for me. That is what being an entrepreneur is all about. Using your ideas not your money.

As an entrepreneur your scarcest resource is time. So you need to think, *leverage*, and get other people, websites, contacts, resources, money, businesses working for you without your direct involvement. Let LinkedIn be your website, let them pay for all the technical IT work, let them set up millions of people to connect to.

Market research

Before you start selling you should have clarified the market that you are approaching and best pricing policy. When you have done this remember that market research is not a one-off activity. It happens with every sale, enquiry and click on your website. You continually hone and change your offer to meet customer needs in a way that will make you most profit. That builds a strong element of safety into your business.

In writing business plans would-be entrepreneurs often estimate sales. When they come into contact with the real world they find the market does not behave as rationally as they thought. They start to realize how illogical people are and how strong brand loyalty is. Often, reaching that market can also present problems.

You need to address these issues before you start selling.

Streetwise promotion

Promotion is informing a prospective customer about and then persuading them to take up your offer. This covers branding, the building of a consistent identity and set of values associated with your offer. In practice, it might mean wearing printed Polo shirts bearing your company name and logo (sell them to get others to promote you), car stickers, websites, directory listings, sponsorships, giving free talks. The list is as endless as the ideas you can generate. I have found that trying different methods is the most effective way to truly find out what works best. Then stick to it.

Streetwise selling

Promotional activity may, if you are lucky, get customers to contact you. Winners, though, don't like to wait, they like to get a head start over their competitors. So I suggest that you get on your phone and you get in your car and talk to as many people as possible.

Here is a simple (because selling is simple) process to follow that will lead to success.

1 Before you make contact, ensure that you are contacting a worthwhile prospect.

2 Before you make contact ensure you are in an enthusiastic, motivated, positive mood. Be prepared for more rejection than acceptance.

3 Before you make contact ensure you know all the benefits of your offer. Here I mean the benefits of owning the product, not a listing of its features.

4 Develop rapport with the person. People need to buy you before buying your offer.

5 Ask questions to find out their personal needs.

6 Do more listening than talking.

7 Tell the prospect about the benefits offered by your product which match their needs. Do not mention benefits that do not match their needs.

8 Ask them if they agree it meets their needs.

9 If they pause, probe or make objections, address their concerns.

10 Ask for their business.

Remember, as an entrepreneur you have a scarcity of resources so always use creativity to leverage your efforts. For example, a client visit is selling to one person in an hour; a free talk might be selling to 100 people in the same time.

Networking

Networking groups have spread like mushrooms around the UK and the world; so they obviously work for a lot of people. Basically their formula is simple. They meet typically very early in the morning, once a week, all stand up and introduce themselves to each other and try to refer their contacts to each other. Thus the contact database is far bigger than the membership. They will let only one person in from each professional area to avoid conflicts of interest. Some will insist that if you can't make the meeting you have to send someone else. For this they can charge about £500 per annum. I have met many people who have won much business via networking groups; they clearly work.

I network everywhere I go, I did it from when I was a child and never attended a course on it, or paid someone to network for me. I have always been successful at it and made countless clients and long-term friends through it. I just cheat and consider everywhere to be a free networking club.

To share that success is easy. Ask yourself when you meet a stranger: 'What do they do that I like and what do they do that I don't like?' Trust me, they will feel the same, so just do it first:

* Have a genuine interest in meeting people.
* Have an open mind.
* Think more about what you can do for them than what they can do for you.
* Realize that good rapport with three people is more valuable than a passing acquaintance with 30.

Online selling

Websites, links on other people's websites, ezines, SEOs... Internet marketing is a big subject covered in the specialist press: the web provides a vast range of cost effective, efficient, non-stop marketing potential. Exploit it but be wary of trying to become the expert, it is just too much to learn.

Streetwise marketing

The biggest spend when you start your own business is usually marketing. Every advertiser is ready to take money off you. However, the true entrepreneur is creative and wins new business without a budget.

How to gain new business without a budget

I once met the Marketing Director of a major British plc, told him about the business I was building up and asked his advice.

He asked, 'What budget do you have?' I replied, 'I don't have a budget.' 'Well you can't do any marketing then,' was his response. Actually I could probably get you more business for the price of an hour's consultation than he could with a £10,000 budget. So read on.

Entrepreneurship is about doing things differently, better and more efficiently, with new ideas, imagination and innovation. It's about changing the world for the better and receiving profit for doing it. As a start-up you are in a race to breakeven point and what makes you faster is cutting unnecessary expenses.

Whatever your business, I can guarantee that there are at least 50 ways to promote it for free and 50 ways for a token amount. There will even be ways in which you can be paid to promote it. One good idea is usually enough.

What exactly is streetwise marketing and how does it work?

Streetwise marketing is about low cost, no cost or receiving an income for your marketing. It starts before the business does. You need to have a passion, drive and energy for what you are about to launch. All the articles, books and seminars tell you this is essential. This is true, but that alone is not enough!

People part with cash to satisfy a need that they have, not to make your dreams come true. Actually they don't care what your goals and dreams are. Do you care what my dreams are? What motivates me to write this book? Or are you focused on 'what is in it for you'?

The streetwise marketer starts by asking: 'What do I keep hearing and/or observing people say that they want and will pay for, which I can provide?'

When you get answers you then match them to what you have a passion and the enthusiasm to provide, NOT THE OTHER WAY AROUND.

The next stage

The streetwise marketer then asks: 'What is so special about what I offer in the eyes of the prospective customer?'

When you have a good answer ask: 'How can I reach this market without spending money?'

You are now on the road to riches.

Surf the web or attend any networking group and you find that most people don't do it this way, which means that you will now have an easy path to prosperity.

If you have to spend all your money developing your ideas and products so that come launch time the coffers are empty, worry not.

So you want some examples of answers to the last question above? Let me give you some methods that work for me. First, you are reading one!

* I sell books, booklets and audio CDs, rather than give out brochures. Whatever you are doing, this is likely to be an option for you too.
* Providing an electronic magazine (ezine) text and video is essential.
* I give free talks to customers with an audience but no budget; you can too. You will sell products and services, win referrals and gain new subscriptions to your ezine. Don't go to networking events, offer to talk at them. They will market you to all their members before the event has even started.
* Offer related online businesses a commission for every one of your products they sell, rather than pay them for advertising. There is no cost to them or you, you both make money without risk.

There are many, many more ideas that will work for you; get started now. The path to success means applying simple ideas and following the easy path instead of the one everyone else is following.

Or, if you prefer I could give you the mobile number of the Marketing Director I met!

This section focuses on the value of questions, offering 100 tried and tested questions to help you increase sales.

Question: *How many professionals does it take to service my requirements?*

Answer: *How many can you afford?*

Sales tips: *Always look to increase sales to a customer. Sell more to existing customers.*

Questions focus the mind of the person being asked. They determine which 'files' in our unconscious are accessed. For example, if I asked you the name of your first school that file would be searched for and when found the name would pop into your conscious mind. Questions also determine our mood, how we feel, by triggering memories and associations. How would you feel if you had just won the lottery? They are very powerful and it is hard to resist their influence. Try not to answer the following questions:

1 10 + 2 = ?
2 Stockholm is the capital of?
3 A collie is a breed of?

Chances are that you are thinking of 12 Swedish dogs.

See the power? It is that easy. I asked you to resist answering and gave you boring, meaningless content. Imagine the increase of power without those two elements.

All of the questions in this section are used regularly by very successful sales people to great effect. We could explain why and go in to great detail. Instead I suggest that you just try the questions with the knowledge that they work. Remember though, English is a language where how you say a word will have an effect, so ask with passion, meaning, interest, respect, enthusiasm, whatever is appropriate.

You will note that most of the 100 questions are to be asked of yourself. This is because it is mainly you who holds yourself back from achieving your potential. You are the constant in all of your sales contacts.

Nearly all prospects will present you, metaphorically speaking, with a silver platter piled high with bundles of £20 notes, to which you can help yourself. All you have to do is listen and take some when invited to.

Converting prospects to customers is easy, they have always been ready to spend money. People like spending money, in fact they are obsessed with it. As credit is less an option these days, you must focus on people with real cash to spend.

They are out there, just waiting for you to get your act together and communicate your message clearly, with enthusiasm, and match it to their needs.

Asking good quality questions then, at the appropriate time is essential to achieve your sales potential. Start with yourself questioning motivation, focus, goal setting, deciding on the best approach.

Having good answers to these types of questions is essential before progressing to your prospects. The rewards of using good quality questions are:

* Controlling the conversation.
* Letting the other person talk more.
* Obtaining information.
* Obtaining decision and commitment.
* Putting the future customer into a buying mood.
* Generating attention and interest.
* Qualifying the buyer.
* Establishing rapport.
* Checking out your assumptions.
* Eliminating or differentiating from the competition.
* Demonstrating that you are listening.
* Helping you to listen.
* Building credibility.
* Knowing the customers and their business.
* Identifying needs.
* Identifying decision makers, influencers, processes and styles.
* Identifying NLP and other patterns of prospects.
* Finding hot buttons.
* Triggering positive associations.
* Obtaining personal information.
* Closing the sale.

* Testing if the sale can be closed.
* Generating other sales leads.

These 100 questions have been researched from successful entrepreneurs and sales professionals to be the ones that have greatest effect.

Ten questions that test your sales and marketing plan

1 Do I know exactly why I am doing this?
2 Is this the best route towards my goals?
3 What would happen if everything went to plan?
4 What would happen if everything did not go to plan?
5 Am I working to my or someone else's goals?
6 Who can I help achieve their goals?
7 If I had a better set of objectives, what would they be?
8 Who can help me achieve my goals?
9 What is special about what I offfer?
10 What will I wish I had done two hours from now?

Ten questions that get you focused

1 What would make me happiest if I achieved it today?
2 Who would benefit most by what I offer?
3 Where are the quickest results to be found?
4 What is the most valuable thing I can do right now?
5 What action should I take now?
6 What question would I like to know the answer to?
7 Who am I letting down by not calling them now?
8 What or who is closest to making me money?
9 What are my priorities?
10 Can I spend more time with prospects offering higher returns?

Ten questions to make you feel great and fired up

1 What three things are really great in my life right now?
2 What would I spend an extra £1,000 on right now?
3 What gift can I give myself?

4 What motivational music could I play on the way to work?
5 What would I treat myself to if I hit target this month?
6 What are my six greatest ever successes in sales?
7 How much is even one good lead potentially worth to me?
8 Would I like to be rich? Why exactly?
9 What would fire me up if I achieved it in the next 15 minutes?
10 What fuels my burning desire to succeed?

Ten questions that increase efficiency

1 How can I do what I do for more people with less work and for a better price?
2 What will I do better next time because of this experience?
3 What resources could I leverage better?
4 What is my most unproductive time in the day?
5 What is a better way to do this?
6 What can I change to move faster?
7 How can I save time?
8 What do the best performers in my market do differently from me?
9 If I employed me, what would I have me focus on?
10 Who do I know that has good ideas?

Ten questions that help at cold calling

1 Who haven't I called recently?
2 What different approach is worth trying?
3 What would I respond positively to if someone called me?
4 Who are the ten people I would most want business from?
5 Who could help me?
6 Who holds the budget?
7 Who is most worth talking to?
8 What is the ideal customer profile I am looking for?
9 What can I say that is different and gets attention fast?
10 What can make my phone call memorable to the other party?

Ten questions that get to the core

1 What is the hidden opportunity here?
2 What could go wrong that I can prepare for now?
3 How motivated am I really?
4 Do you have any questions?
5 What did I notice about myself today?
6 What is really important to my prospects?
7 What motivates me the most?
8 What metaphors is he/she using?
9 What problem can I solve?
10 Is he/she using more visual, auditory or feeling words?

Ten questions that improve your approach

1 Am I selling from the customer's perspective?
2 Do I know at least 30 benefits of a prospect choosing me?
3 Are my prices high enough?
4 Am I providing what people want to buy in the way they want to buy it?
5 Do I truly believe that what I offer adds value to customers?
6 Am I using all my advantages to the full?
7 Have I asked my prospects what approach works with them?
8 What is my weakest area in sales that I can work on?
9 In what way can I be better?
10 What can I do to excel?

Ten questions that gather information

1 Can you think of one special time when you purchased something and everything went really well?
2 Describe to me the perfect supplier?
3 What is your ultimate objective?
4 Tell me, what headaches have you got, that I might be the Anadin™ for?
5 Fancy a cappuccino?
6 How can I help you?
7 How interested are you on a scale from 1 to 10?

8 What can I say that you would like to hear?

9 What would I have to do to win your confidence?

10 Can I ask you for some advice?

Ten questions that move you towards a deal

1 What would you do if you were me?

2 What would we have to do to be even better than your current suppliers?

3 Do you have a 'contingencies' budget?

4 What is the key question you need to ask me?

5 What is the one thing I could offer that would get you interested?

6 If I could address all the issues you have, would you go ahead and place an order with me?

7 How can we best move forward?

8 What is your decision making process?

9 What, if anything, stops you from going ahead?

10 What could I do now to secure an order from you?

Ten questions that close the deal

1 Shall we go ahead then?

2 Are you in a position to go ahead if you like what I have to say?

3 Who else do you know who might be interested in this?

4 If I agree to what you ask can you agree a deal now?

5 Do you want the standard or deluxe version?

6 You agree that this represents real value for money, don't you?

7 Can you see all the benefits to you of what I am offering?

8 Is there anything important to you that I have not covered?

9 How does that sound?

10 Are all your criteria met by what I have proposed?

Getting LinkedIn

Whatever your business, social media is no longer a choice – it is compulsory. If you are not getting sales and other business leads through social media, you are missing out big time.

LinkedIn, Ecademy and Twitter are the key services for the UK business community. Many people though are baffled by it all, others get to fill in their basic profile and then don't take it any further. Only the minority take full advantage and reap the rewards.

These services are free and offer the best promotion your business can get. Someone else is paying the IT staff to connect you to who you need connecting to. They are getting you 'Googled' every day. The idea is summed up in the title of Ecademy founder Penny Powers' book: *Know Me, Like Me, Follow Me*. When you know what you are doing your time is really leveraged and you have a major resource working for you.

Some time back I contacted a sales trainer, Paul Routley, on Ecademy and offered him a commission to introduce me to customers. He produced more sales leads than my full-time staff. He is also a trainer with LinkedIn, and he now teaches in my 100K Club.

If you don't know the 'hows', find someone who does, and get them to tell you. Buy a book, go on a course, get a coach, surf for YouTube videos. Whatever the route, do it and get it done. Then connect with me on LinkedIn and I will help you grow.

success mentor

Entrepreneurship skills can take many years to learn and hone to effectiveness. The good news is that you can use the years of experience of others rather than your own. I have included many golden nuggets here. I update this list on my Twitter feeds as I develop them. Don't be arrogant or opinionated, study people with successful businesses and the best practices will become clear.

But knowledge is not power until it is acted upon. So do not just have knowledge of these golden nuggets, instead focus on applying them and making them habitual. Also make a habit of being observant, notice what works and what does not from businesses around you. Learn fast from any mistakes you make, don't keep doing them.

Read up on successful businesses and business people. Before you try anything, find someone who had tried it and ask what results they got.

Only buy at bargain prices

If it is not a bargain, haggle, shop around, do without, take other routes, wait until it is a bargain. In negotiation time and waiting is, more often than not, a powerful influencing tool so never be in a hurry when buying. In practice, when we shop around, we are inevitably then offered the same or a similar thing for a better deal. Refer to the life stories of Paul Getty and Warren Buffet and see how these billionaires have mastered this principle.

Know the difference between an investment and a cost

Poorly performing entrepreneurs do not understand the difference between a cost and an investment. Investments are things that you want more of, because they make an eventual and regular contribution to profit. Costs, on the other hand, reduce profit and need keeping to a minimum without adversely affecting operations. Look at your own business in the last month and differentiate costs from investments.

Turn your garage into an office

When studying entrepreneurs I hear time and again something that sounded quite strange to me at first. Running a business profitably is all about keeping costs down. There is a clue in this. Business is simple and runs to the equation: Sales – Costs = Profits.

The wise also realize that there is a difference between good and bad costs. A good cost is one that directly increases sales or the potential for sales. Any other cost is something that threatens you. At some point during a business life cycle cash inflows will go down for whatever reason. If your minimum cost base is less than your competitors' you will probably outlast them. The more cost the quicker you will be threatened.

I buy my PCs, laptops, carpets, furniture second hand or from places like IKEA, which are focused on functionality rather than charging premiums for designer labels. Impress others with your profit level, rather than expensive habits.

Mind the pennies and the pounds will look after themselves.

Live within your means

I have noticed that most people instead of accumulating wealth are working their way out of debt. Therefore, as part of the club I run, I try to help people reorganize their lives with some sensible financial planning, according to their goals. The big spenders are not the rich, they know how to keep hold of their money and not be tempted against their best interests. Big spenders tend to be people doing it on credit who are satisfying their short-term desires for a much increased long-term cost. This 'lunacy' created the credit crunch and, as people, businesses and even government are all paying off debts, who is going to increase spending to fuel a recovery? Be wise, be prudent and thrifty.

Cash is king

When it comes to accounting, entrepreneurs seem to focus their attention on cash flow. They see their business in cash flow terms even when it becomes larger. They concentrate on increasing cash in and reducing cash out. When it comes to the balance sheet they think of assets as things that produce income, and liabilities as things that cost them money. Accountants see property, fixtures and fittings, and motor vehicles as assets. As these things cost money to run entrepreneurs see them as liabilities. Key people are not valued in the accounts. The Virgin Group's accounts will show Richard Branson's PC as an asset but not him. If I had him advising my enterprises I would consider him to be a very valuable asset that I would use to the full.

Recruit the best and set them up to be outstanding

Make it difficult to get a job with your company, through a rigorous recruitment process. Then don't try to get the best staff by relying on paying the highest salaries. The harder it is to get a job with your company the more elitist it will become and the more demand there will be for people to work for you. When they get through this procedure they will also value the job far more and be far less inclined to leave. People naturally value things according to how much effort it took to achieve them. Think of the organizations you know that you consider to be leading in their field and then look at how they recruit.

How do you make yours a tough recruitment process? Various ways: many interviews, panel interviews, aptitude and personality tests, assessment days, rigorous and professional interviewing and selection. The best way is to use an outside organization to carry out the short-list assessments. This, in itself, sends a message to would-be applicants of just how seriously you take your recruitment process. It ups the value of a job with you in their eyes. I have found that the better employers often pay less than their average counterparts. I conclude that professional recruitment is an investment and salaries are mainly a cost. Identify the exact profile of the people you wish to recruit and keep looking until you have found them.

Train an elite team

Training is often something that is considered important but not urgent and thus keeps getting postponed. Again this comes back to my earlier observation of the most successful entrepreneurs balancing long-term and short-term needs. Training, when selected carefully, is not a cost but an investment with a long-term return. It gives you an edge over your competition. It can make you more efficient in any of the functions of your business. It is also motivational to staff. American entrepreneurs have a far greater record here than their British counterparts. Americans spend enormous amounts, by British standards, both corporately and individually.

Training return is limited by the quality of the staff being trained. You should initially spend time clarifying your recruitment policy and processes. Recruit the best and you will also get the bonus of a better return from the training you give them.

Establish a corporate and team identity and culture

It is clear that entrepreneurial companies which really go places identify a strong team and corporate culture early on, and then recruit people whose personalities match that culture and identity. This they put before job competencies, as skill training will be a lot easier than personality changing. There seems to be the view that if people really fit in with the team the company can easily train them in any skills they are missing.

Have a microscope and a telescope

Focus on what is immediately in front of you and on the horizon. Entrepreneurs of any type and at any level of financial success tend to talk about what they are going to do rather than what they have achieved. This includes entrepreneurs already beyond retirement age. Their focus is clearly future orientated and perhaps this gives a clue as to how they see new opportunities and don't get bogged down in old ways of doing things. It also casts light on how they manage to keep positive when experiencing failures. The failures as soon as they are past become out of focus, literally. Obviously we can learn important lessons from the past but often successful entrepreneurs beat those who started with so much more experience, knowledge and resources. This implies that whereas good can come from experience, it can also limit us.

Catch the success virus

Destiny will deliver to you a certain amount of good and bad luck. I don't know about you but I want more than my fair share, so I fix the odds in my favour. Here is how.

How much do you want to be a millionaire? If I asked you to take a risk on the roulette wheel, bet £1,000 and if 22 comes up I will give you £1 million, otherwise you lose, would you take the bet?

If I said gamble £10,000 and if anything other than 22 comes up I will pay you £1 million would you now take the bet?

If I said that if anything but 22 comes up I will pay you £10 million, but if 22 comes up I will take all your worldly possessions, would you take the bet?

What do your answers and thinking tell you about your attitude to risk?

Let me tell you what a self-made millionaire would do. Find another game where they could determine the stakes, the odds and have a strong influence on the outcome, to play money-making games without even being there. Entrepreneurs don't play roulette, they have not got time for games of chance. Losers play roulette and gamble. Entrepreneurs design their own game, reduce the odds of them losing, increase the odds of them winning and cover for the downside. The entrepreneur would either receive a royalty on inventing the game or own the casino!

So what do you have to change in order to become an entrepreneur?

Success is contagious, hang around it and you will catch it!

Make negative words illegal

In one of my training sessions I put up two flipcharts and ask the delegates to write positive words on one flipchart and negative words on the other.

Then I got them to talk to each other in various contexts using the words from one of the boards alternately. The result is simple and dramatic. The delegates who are hearing the negative words rapidly decline in mood. Those hearing positive words rapidly begin to smile, laugh and are full of energy, and all that is associated with positive thinking.

Words that we hear generate internal pictures and sounds which in turn, determine our feelings. Therefore, what I do and have done for many clients is to get them to do two things. This tip is free, simple and always works.

1 Surround the workplace walls with positive pictures, suggestions, quotes and words.
2 Open a negative word box. Every time someone uses a negative word they have to put £10 into a box and then they have to repeat what they said but in a positive way.

Be decisive but explore all the options and implications first

When you can you must learn how to wait and be patient, wait for something good, the right deal to turn up. Ascertain anything that could go wrong and make your decision on as much information as you can. Take as much time making important decisions as you can, but don't hang around too long or opportunity will be lost.

Be flexible, see from multiple perspectives

Keep trying different approaches until you are successful. Looking at a challenge from a different point of view often produces ideas. Ask other people their opinion. Look at everything first from the customer's point of view.

Think ahead

Always think ahead and think about anything that could go wrong in the future. This is deliberately making yourself think negatively. Now you have time on your side to work out what to do. You can even take it a step further and figure out how you could benefit from the event transpiring. Everything that happens in business has a positive side and the easiest way to exploit it is to think ahead of time.

Play Monopoly® for real money

I find it interesting that Bill Gates in his younger days was an avid player of Monopoly®. I have heard many wealthy entrepreneurs refer to the principles that need to be applied to this game. Looking closer we can learn and apply a lot of these principles. For example, certain players will always go for the dark blue (e.g. Mayfair and Park Lane in the London edition) set, but these people very rarely win.

In fact, more often than not, the winner is the person who 'owns' the orange set, where the balance of investment to return is not too hard to build, and the returns are worthwhile. It does not cripple you as you are building it up. It allows you to build some wealth and then from that higher standpoint the dark blue set seems a worthwhile investment.

The brown set is handy to generate cash flow but with only two properties it would take forever to generate reasonable wealth. The stations offer four properties with a reasonable, frequent return without any building costs. You will never win on this set alone but they can finance you as you go along, keeping the cash flowing.

Chance and Community Chest again is realistic to life. The wise player knows all the cards that can come up and sets something aside for the worst scenario. The best way to learn from Monopoly® is to play with friends for real money. That way the lessons will be logged into your unconscious as you are getting real business experience.

Always have a plan B and a plan C

Successful entrepreneurs are always thinking ahead and considering every scenario. The biographies of Aristotle Onassis,

John D Rockefeller and Paul Getty clearly show this trait again and again. So often when their opponents thought they had been caught out, these entrepreneurs would clearly show that they had made contingency plans for exactly the situation they had got into. And do it for two moves ahead. Onassis, for example, was pursued by the CIA, for good reasons, when he admitted to organizing a strike in the Hamburg boatyard that was working on his ship. The CIA case failed. Another time he was whaling off the Chilean coast and the CIA arranged for Onassis's boats to be impounded. It later transpired, whereas the CIA thought they had ruined Onassis, that his insurance contract with Lloyds had a clause in it predicting this possibility with a very large payoff. He made an incredible profit by foreseeing this possible scenario.

So in your business ask yourself what could go wrong in the next three months. When you have that information, ask what you can do now to prepare for it, or even make opportunity from it. To be really safe, prepare for your plan B going wrong with a plan C ready.

Harness your whole concentration upon one goal

If you have five things to achieve, the more you can do them sequentially the more success you will have. Attending to five things at once usually means that none of them is achieved. If you focus your mind on one goal your thinking can, by definition, be much clearer and you will arrive at quicker, better answers.

Provide what people want to buy

Entrepreneurs have a real passion for their ideas and products. This does not mean that the buying public will. Products have to be sold and people buy things when they perceive a need for them relative to competitors. What people want or should want can be very different from what they will part with money for.

The best products are those that were initiated by seeing a need in the market place and then supplying it, not the other way around. People pay for what they want to have, not what you want to give them. You can influence what they want though.

Get free publicity and advertising

Before you raise finance to spend a small fortune on promoting your business, seek and exploit all the free ways first. You can write articles for online and offline periodicals, give radio or television interviews, give a free seminar at an association. There are always lots of ways depending on what you are offering. Find at least five before you spend on advertising.

Spread the word

The most effective marketing is word of mouth and personal recommendation. It is the most reliable and the cheapest. People who are recommended are also less likely to haggle on price, being already convinced of quality and service.

If in doubt raise prices

There are four reasons why, if you are in doubt, you should raise your prices.

1 Most people associate price with quality.
2 It can give you more profit even if volume drops.
3 Volume may go up.
4 It will give you valuable information on price elasticity.

Be in the right place at the right time

Having studied entrepreneurs in detail, it is clear that there are certain golden rules that are discussed throughout this book. There are traits that allow an enterprise to be launched and developed from the first stages to profit. The really big stars seem to have an additional ability to be in the right place at the right time relative to their talents. Many artists, for example, die penniless only for their work to be acclaimed as masterpieces much too late for them to benefit from it.

To be in the right place at the right time as a business entrepreneur is to not invent and take your goods to market, but to do it the other way around. In other words, find out what people might have a need for if it were to exist and then go away and invent it. That is how you make sure that you are in the right place at the right time.

These good times keep coming around: you are in one now; change always creates new needs. The fastest to recognize and exploit these needs make a fortune.

Think opportunity

Always look for opportunity. For example, when negotiating with a supplier can you put any other business their way? How about more favourable terms in return for their brochures in your office, or a link on your website?

Ask a lot of 'why' questions

'Why' questions get you in the habit of challenging the current status quo and this process leads to you seeing opportunities. The opportunities were always there, it is just that you could not see them until you started to ask some 'why' questions.

Move fast

Put deadlines before quality. Get something to market fast then continually improve it. If you wait for perfection the market will have moved on. Microsoft® has spent years developing and improving a PC operating system for common use. Their earlier versions were absolutely riddled with bugs, breakdowns and totally meaningless error messages. They still offered more than their competitors and customer feedback led to enhancements.

Business is about deadlines. This is doubly hard for an entrepreneur getting established with limited resources. Meeting deadlines is an essential step to success.

Keep it simple

This is a very well-worn principle in business and I came across it being put into active use by all the entrepreneurs I know of. Business is not an intellectual exercise, don't make it one.

Do what has to be done

As your own boss you are free to decide what to do each day. Most of us, naturally, will focus on what we want to do. Instead, ask yourself what needs to be done with priority in order to meet your goals, and focus on doing the answer.

Keep to your strength areas, you have advantages here

Know your strength areas and keep to them. Everything else look to delegate, as soon as possible. Your time is precious and in short supply. Maintain its usefulness at maximum output. Doing the accounts yourself, for example, is not a thrifty habit, it is a lavish one. What will take you a week and not be done properly can be done in two hours by a professional accountant.

Take a trip to the US of A

The United States is the greatest source of new ideas being put into practice in the world. Their society was largely founded on the principle of entrepreneurship. Many people became millionaires in Europe by seeing great ideas in action in the USA and bringing them home. Many more were inspired by just how creative and imaginative Americans are. Nowhere in the world are people encouraged and free to dream more than in the USA. If you want an idea of how big Americans can dream take a visit to the Walt DisneyWorld® Resort in Florida and the next day visit the Kennedy Space Center as I did. Think of all the big companies now in the world that have come from the internet age. How many can you think of that are not American?

Googling away – a dozen sub-mindsets

Here's a list of a dozen behaviours/patterns/beliefs/attitudes that come from Larry and Sergey, the founders of Google – they were billionaires before the age of 31!!

* Use only free publicity.
* Use 20 per cent of your time exploring your passion.
* PPP – Prepare for Potential Problems.
* Get the audience first, then sell to them.
* Go where the money is being spent.
* Think differently.
* Partnership for leverage.
* Don't be clever, judge the clever.
* Generate trickles, the flow and flood will come.
* Learn from other people's mistakes.
* See the future and plan for it.
* Competition is your way to success.

7

going for it!

You have found out your profile, matched it to a suitable opportunity and designed a plan of action. You have identified specific opportunities you can go for. You have even taken on board some quality advice from experience on how best to run your business. Well, the time has come to stop thinking and take action. Take action, listen to feedback, react to that feedback, take more action.

You must focus on what the business needs you to do. Not what you want to do. As your own boss you must be the strictest, toughest person to work for.

Remember the idea of a business is to put more money in your pocket, not out of it. Find ways to achieve sales and profits with a minimum of risk to yourself. If you ever encounter an obstacle get around it by having a great spark of entrepreneurial inspiration and innovation.

Two of the most common questions I am asked by aspiring entrepreneurs are:

1 How do you get started while providing for yourself and perhaps a family?
2 How can you raise enough finance to get your business off the ground if the bank turns you down?

Focus

In working out their goals, many people seem to focus on houses, holidays, cars, etc. It is more effective to focus on financial freedom as your goal. All the other things will come anyway. You are financially free when you have created enough wealth so that your income from it, without depleting capital, is sufficient to live on. In this situation you never have to worry about money, ever again. Luxury goods deplete wealth and should never hamper your progress towards financial freedom or take it away from you.

You tend to get what you focus on and the material things can be achieved by raising mortgages, loans and credit cards. I think that having a lovely house with a larger mortgage, a car on loan and a holiday paid for by credit card is celebrating success before it has happened and does not lead to happiness. This is conditioning your mind to reward yourself without success, and this sets up bad habits that at best will hold you back, at worst put you out of business.

So have houses, cars, holidays as part of your dream building, but make sure that you reward yourself when you can really afford them by paying cash and by remaining financially free. Once you are financially free you never want to risk losing this position. Focusing on being financially free is more supportive to running your business. It keeps your mind on cutting costs, making sales, creating new ideas, growing and investing; this is what counts. Your goals are the driving force that will keep your motivation fired up, whatever the conditions.

Goals can seem sometimes too big a target, too far off. The thing to remember is that a goal is like a house: it is made up of individual parts, every brick you build is one step closer to the house. Every step forward in your business is a step in the right direction. Always focus on achieving the next step. It will be easy to focus on and not be an overwhelming target. We can see clearly what is close to us. Do something every day to take you closer to your goal.

The success decision

Entrepreneurship is a state of mind, an attitude and a decision. So one of the secrets is taking control of your thoughts, making them work towards your goals. Most people are a slave of their thoughts, their thoughts take them randomly through life. They feel depressed and they don't even know why. Feeling good is a thought. Don't believe me, try this.

To learn you should pay more attention, from challenging what you already know, do or believe in to seeing what else comes in. Changing some of the routine things we do teaches us how to break patterns and allow in new choices. We can think in a different way.

Motivation

If I set you the challenge of making a million in the next three months could you do it?

If you had three months in which to make a million, or you would lose all contact with your family and friends, could you do it?

Most people say no to the first and yes to the second. If this is you, my next question is what changed?

See, motivation is easy. It all depends on your desire and how much you want something.

Customer focus

Many people I have coached and trained in sales have needed their focus changing, from their commission to the needs of the prospect. Prospects will tell you their needs freely and provide you with commercial opportunities. If you are walking in with a specific product to sell, you will focus on how to move your prospect's conversation to your offer. It is better selling to just listen and then offer something that truly addresses their needs. People looking for commission focus on their offer. There is no 'empathy bond' created, the bond that transfers knowledge.

Some of you stop growing because you believe you have not got enough brains. Hey, use other people's brains! Business is a team sport. Knowledge is easy to acquire. Anything you want to know just type it in the search engine of your web browser. It is that simple.

Sales channels

There is always more than one way to sell your merchandise. Here are some avenues for your consideration.
* Set up a group of sales agents.
* Employ commissioned sales representatives.
* Organize other companies to be resellers.
* Give free talks, presentations or demonstrations.
* Offer your products to a network marketing company or set one up yourself.

Free resources around you

You are surrounded by great wealth, all is available for you to use freely. Have you taken your share yet? Here are some sources for consideration:
* local library
* friends
* personal contacts
* government offices
* tax rebate if starting on low income
* potential suppliers
* brains of friends
* living room
* location
* competitors
* potential suppliers.

What stops you going for it?

Barriers to entry in any particular industry vary but the most common responses I get from people who have not started yet are: supporting my family and the mortgage, lack of finance, lack of suitable staff, lack of an established name. They are all excuses for not overcoming fear of some sort. Recognize this, and identify and work on those fears.

Finance raising for the entrepreneurial firm is hard. Retained profits are clearly the main source and thus there is even more of a case for thrift, to make sure every penny made can be reinvested. Many entrepreneurs are caught in the dilemma of having a full order book, which they are turning away, due to lack of finance to produce.

Fear is the biggest stopper: fear of losing your house, poverty, criticism, failure. My boss once said to me: 'If the pressure comes on get your head down and work.' A good technique for two reasons:

1 If your mind is occupied with working you have not got spare capacity for worry.
2 By taking action it is fairly obvious that your work is going to progress you beyond your current challenges.

Pricing

I have noticed many times that when considering price, people will focus more on a discount than they do on the absolute price. They will also judge quality from the original price not the discounted one. Their attention is on how much money is off. So if you want £25 for an item, ask for £35 and offer them a special £10 discount. Their mind immediately focuses on the £10 saving on a £35 level of quality item. It is an illusion, as the basis for the £35 price was not established in the first place.

So when you are buying, only consider the asking price. Be wary of making judgements on what the price used to be. If there were buyers at this price they would not be offering a discount!

One thing at a time

Be wary of having five great ideas and going for all of them. Focusing on one, making it work and then moving on to the next is a much more practical strategy destined for success.

If you are starting a new enterprise, that very newness can put off both potential customers and suppliers. The latter look for cash payments until you have established yourself. To a potential customer, your being new means that your service is more unpredictable than an established player. Naturally, how important these points are depends on your type of business.

The beauty about owning your own business is that you can run it the way you want. Business history is full of radical ideas, well out of the ordinary, that worked. There are even more failures. The ideas have got to work.

Don't give up

Many entrepreneurs who have made a great fortune claim to have struggled for years. In fact, weeks before their big breakthrough came they debated with themselves regularly on giving up. They often think that if they had given up, they would have never known just how near they were to a fortune. So often great success is just around the corner.

Networking

Think about all the people you could possibly contact to get your sales off the ground. Learn and use 'Ecademy' and 'LinkedIn' and then you will have as many useful contacts as you want.

Know what you are up against?

Carry out your own survey of competitors. Phone them.
* How many rings before they answered?
* How pleasant out of ten was the greeting?
* Were you left hanging on?

* Did they ask your name or number?
* Did they really want your business?

If you make sure that your employees perform better than the above, you will rise above them.

The most crucial resource in any business is its people. At the beginning, one mistake and the enterprise can be out for the count before it has had its fair chance. Therefore people, as a resource, have to be managed effectively. The entrepreneur has to take total responsibility.

Practicality of raising money

Good entrepreneurs apply their creativity to minimizing the financial resources they will need to get their venture underway. They will live on a survival budget, work all hours from home, convert the garage and buy second hand. This way they can slowly build up sales with a minimum of overheads, learning as they go, getting the business model right, and grow from there.

Sometimes, though, depending on the nature of the venture this method might work but raising significant finance can make what would happen in five years happen in one year. Books on business will advise you that there are two main sources of finance: debt or equity. This means that you get a loan and pay interest or sell shares in return for a cash investment. In practice, both sources have benefits and disadvantages. For many entrepreneurs, post credit crunch, the loan route will be limited unless they have considerable assets to secure the loan.

Do not be naïve. If you walk in to a bank with a fantastic plan for a business, you will probably be turned down. At some point you will be asked how much equity you have in your house; this is their primary interest. Despite what has happened, the UK still has a finance industry based upon property. This secures their loan if the business fails. As their statistics will clearly indicate, only one in a hundred businesses survives the first year. So expect to be rejected; they, after all, will not share in your capital gain if you make it big. Why should they finance your dream? There are, however, sometimes schemes available such as guaranteed security from the government for a loan.

That is where venture capitalists come in. These can be private investors, known as business angels, or institutions. If you go down this route your main cost can be all the time you spend researching, developing, visiting, presenting and negotiating with these people. You have to become an expert in something you will probably only do once. That is why I recommend going to a medium to large firm of accountants or lawyers which specialize in this area. They usually work on a percentage of money raised. They also do a great deal of the work and can give good advice on a whole range of things such as patents and contracts.

Now I am going to tell you the streetwise ways to finance your business that the business school books don't tell you about.

Factoring/invoice discounting

Factoring is a great idea for growth companies with continually increasing needs for working capital. Basically the concept is simple. The finance company will give you what is effectively a secured loan on your invoices out. To an entrepreneurial company the debtor balance is always growing and thus always causing more of a strain. Factoring will give you a percentage of your invoices on issue and charge you an overdraft-type interest rate. They will also now provide you with full credit control and legal services. If your business is paying out for contract labour on a weekly basis and being paid on 30 to 90 day terms, factoring can be the difference between being in or out of business. Bear in mind, if you grow your overdraft size automatically goes up with your invoicing level.

Again, look closely at the small print of the agreement you will be signing. They often want personal guarantees and initial deposits, both of which I have negotiated out of a deal in the past so I know that you can achieve the same. Still though only take on customers that are financially sound as the risk is still yours.

Grants and awards

Contact your bank manager, the Department of Trade and Industry, Business Link, the Training and Enterprise Council, the European Commission, your MP, Euro MP, Chamber of Commerce, local networking group, trade or professional association and your accountant for information. Big companies sometimes have a programme to support entrepreneurs: Shell, BT and IBM have done so in the past. There are many grants available particularly if you are set up in a relatively less developed part of the country. They are clearly worth pursuing but sometimes the research and application process can be time consuming with no guaranteed result. Time that could have been spent productively.

Retained contracts

Whatever business you are trying to launch, this method is always worth consideration. The technique basically rests on who will buy from you when you are up and running. Visit prospective customers and sign them up to a contract, where they pay one-third as an initial retainer for you to start work. (You never let them know just how dependent you are on the upfront payment.) Aristotle Onassis was a master of this technique. He started his shipping career by getting a contract for delivery and then taking that to a bank in order to get a loan to buy a ship! Thus he was able to offer collateral.

Supplier credit

When you have worked out your business plan, you will know what you need the money for. If you can negotiate 90-day terms with suppliers this could solve or considerably reduce your financial requirements. Those 90-days will allow you to get your own sales up and running. Find suppliers who need orders. Once you are trading, your suppliers can be kept at bay with promises of future orders. Bear in mind that to pursue their money would, in practice, take at least another 90 days anyway. Ideally, rather than just not pay creditors, negotiate the terms, keeping their goodwill, offering them your long-term business as you grow.

Fast-growth businesses, by definition, need a lot of investment to keep the momentum going. I have been in the situation of having an overloaded order book without the finance to employ the staff to carry out the work. It is a very frustrating and real problem. You turn it away or take the risk of overtrading. That is going bust, caused by trying to keep up with rising sales while cash flow is becoming overstrained.

Contingency payments

Advertise by paying the advertiser commission on sales. For example, instead of buying advertising space, negotiate a deal where the company can market your products for a cut. This way you have no advertising spend and a steady income stream without any incumbent fixed costs. Whatever your product or service, there will be hundreds of webmasters interested in such a proposal. Pick sites which have the type of traffic that would be interested in what you offer.

Supplier funding

This method is producing to order. Market your goods and services whatever they are and produce them to order, thereby avoiding the necessity to manufacture and hold inventory. You may have to work very fast, so make sure you are prepared.

Who else has got an interest in me succeeding?

Ask yourself the above question. When you have the answers, and there will be many, ask yourself how you can use this knowledge to help the enterprise. Issuing shares to family and friends can be better than just asking for loans. This way they participate in the profits if all goes to plan and you do not have a debt if it does not. Later, when raising further venture capital, it could look good to have more than you as a shareholder.

Reverse financing

Another way of solving this demand for funding is to look at the challenge inside out.

In other words, instead of bringing capital into the company, take the company to the capital. You can approach an existing larger company that is well funded, and offer your enterprise together with you as a package. Part of the deal is that they can have majority control and even a formula to buy out your minority interest geared to performance.

This way you can use their corporate resources and infrastructure without any extra spend: they will have an established name, contacts and markets. Your venture is now far more secure and has a far greater chance of success. They have control both of the shareholding and of financial decisions. Therefore their investment too is a lot less risky. It is essential that the partnership is made with an organization that has synergy with your enterprise. Specifically the partnership can further exploit resources that they already have.

You become MD, or whatever your preferred role/skill is, and with your team you make it happen. Another advantage of the small and large companies working together is that a larger organization will have more muscle to help you get through things like recession or other temporary challenges that arise.

This is an ideal option if your objective is a capital gain. You are more interested in the value of your shareholding than the percentage. You could also use this route to sell out and have a significant cash resource for your next venture.

Franchising

Be a franchisor. This way the managers of all the branches effectively bankroll the whole operation. Franchising is a possibility when you have a business model that can be duplicated easily to autonomous units. The main danger is having franchisees who, being owners, want to call the tune all the time. You cannot control a franchisee in the same way as you can control an employed manager. Many small companies have become large this way, without the need to raise large amounts of capital.